ROCKINGHAM COUNTY

NORTH CAROLINA

DEED ABSTRACTS

1785 - 1800

SOUTHERN HISTORICAL PRESS INC

Book Publishers

Abstracted, Compiled and Indexed

by

Irene B. Webster

Please direct all correspondence and orders to:

www.southernhistoricalpress.com
or
SOUTHERN HISTORICAL PRESS, Inc.
PO BOX 1267
375 West Broad Street
Greenville, SC   29601
southernhistoricalpress@gmail.com

ISBN #0-89308-351-8

Printed in the United States of America

FOREWORD

The earliest Will Books and Deed Books of Rockingham County have been restored and rebound by the Archives Division of the North Carolina Department of Art, Culture, and History in Raleigh. Modern Methods of this type of restoration are unbelieveably good; however, what had already been lost could not be restored.

This is the case with Deed Book A. The first eight pages were missing and several of the first and last pages were badly worn before the book was restored. There was damage to a lesser degree in the next four Deed Books abstracted for this volume.

We begin with a fragment of a grant to Honourable William Byrd of 6,000 acres adjoining the 20,000 acres of Col. William Byrd. This is confusing until we read the deed following that grant and it is explained that the son, William, bought the 6,000 acres adjoining the father's grant of 20,000.

"The Land of Eden" was the name given to this unsettled area in 1728 by Col. William Byrd when he served as a Virginia Commissioner on the expedition with the surveyors who "ran the line" between Virginia and North Carolina. For more about this interesting venture, do read "William Byrd's Histories of the Dividing Line betwixt Virginia and North Carolina" which has been published again recently in paperback by Dover Publications. It contains the secret history kept daily on the expedition and the more formal history written later.

Rockingham County was formed from Guilford County in 1785. As with all newly formed counties, it took years to build a court house and establish a sound system of record keeping. Some of the records probably remained in Guilford County for a long time. The thorough search of these earliest records, as required by such a volume as this, has unearthed some genealogical facts and clues that might not otherwise have been found.

Land Grants. Only two were for Revolutionary service--one to Alexander Martin and one to William Hitchcock with James Hunter as his assignee. The earliest of the other grants issued by the secretary of the various governors of the State of North Carolina were "for and in consideration of the sum of Fifty Shillings for every hundred Acres". Beginning in 1788, there was an increasing number of grants "for and in consideration of the sum of ten pounds for every hundred Acres". From about 1793, there were some grants for thirty shillings per one hundred acres. For the sake of brevity, in trying to cover as many years as possible in this volume, the amount has been omitted in the abstracts unless there is a variation from the above amounts.

Hogans Creek. There were and still are two! Lickfork Creek flows into the eastern one. The western one empties into Dan River which weaves diagonally across the county northeasterly.

While the title of the book gives dates 1785 - 1800, there are many 1799 deeds recorded in later Deed Books. It is not explainable that a few 1800 deeds appear in the first book, while the fifth book did not cover all the 1799 deeds.

ACKNOWLEDGMENTS

Appreciation is expressed to:

Irene, Jan and Karen Frye - precocious
and pretty granddaughters, for their help
in preparing the index. This is not their
premiere - in fact, their presence on the
scene was premeditated and prearranged
because of previous help on preceding
presentations.

Mrs. J. Lee McCollum, Jr. Mary Louise
usually has the prescription to prevent
prevailing predicaments, so her help in
preparing a presentable publication with
precision is always predictable; and that
is no prevarication.

TABLE OF CONTENTS

Book A, page 9. Province of N. C.; Gabriel Johnston, Royal Governor to William Byrd 6,000 A in Orange Co. adj Col. Byrd. Mar. 22, 1742.

Book A, page 10. Hon. William Byrd and wife Elizabeth of Charles City Co., Va. to Francis Farley and wife Simon of the Island of Antigua, merchants, for 1,000 pds Lawfull money of Great Britain 26,000 A on both sides Dann R in Orange Co. 20,000 A having been granted to William Byrd Esq. of Charles City Co., Va. and Father of the above named William Byrd Dec. 9, 1728; the other 6,000 having been granted to sd William Byrd, the son, March 22, 1742. Nov. 8, 1755. Proved by Robert Jones Jr.

Book A, page 15. Robert Burton of Granville C. to Allen Gates for $600, 161 A on W side Mayo R adj Isham Sharp, being land bought by sd Burton from Richard Sharp. Apr. 13, 1801. Susan Henderson, Pleasant Henderson.

Book A, page 16. State of N. C. to Charles Gilley, 100 A on Lickfork of Hogans Cr. adj Simon Lovelatty, Hugh Chalice, John Mount. Nov. 8, 1784.

Book A, page 27. (Either 10 pages missing or numbering is changed). State of N. C. to Abner Chinault on S side Dan R. adj his own line, Dudley Porter, William Southerland, Valentine Allen. Dec. 18, 1799.

Book A, page 28. Abraham James, Jacob James & Sharod Brock, Atty for William James, to Nathaniel Harris for 50 pds land on both sides Matrimony Cr. adj his own land. (Date torn). Anher Murphrey, Thos. Hairis, Jesse Hairis.

Book A, page 30. Richard Stubblefield to Wyatt Stubblefield of Caswell Co. for 50 pds 24 A adj Joseph Cloud, Richard Stubblefield, Wyat Stubblefield, Archibald Yarbrough, Joseph C. Thrasher. Apr. 1780. Richard Stubblefield Jr., William Bethell.

Book A, page 31. Archibald Yarbrough and wife Nancy to Wyatt Stubblefield of Caswell Co. for 200 pds 164 A & 130 poles in counties of Rockingham & Caswell on N side of Hogans Cr. Apr. 28, 1787. Richard Stubblefield Junr., William Bethell.

Book A, page 33. State of N. C. to Aron Going 410 A on head of Matrimony Cr. of Dan R and on Papa Cr. of Mayo R adj former line of Samuel Gates and Hamilton's line. May 16, 1787.

Book A, page 35. Christopher Dudley of Roan Co. to John Parker for $105 200 A on Quaqua Cr. Dec. 5, 1800. Philip Trotter, Ransom Dudley, James Wilbone.

Book A, page 36. Samuel Allen to Joseph Allen Jr. for 100 pds 100 A on E side of Hogans Cr. adj Samuel Watt. Aug. 26, 1801. Daniel Allen, John Willson, Soloman Allen.

Book A, page 37. Robert Williams to William Lawson of Person Co. for $2,348.00 776 A on both sides Wolf Island Cr. adj William Bethell, William Russell, John Smith, Hugh Challes, Notty Jordan being tract bought from Richard Marr. Sept. 18, 1801. William Bethell, William Bethell Jr.

Book A, page 38. John Reagon, Atty for James Reagon, to Reubin McDaniel of Stokes Co. for 200 pds 429 A on Nelson Br of Belews Cr adj Absalom Bostick, Joseph Ladd, Hezekiah Cary, John Ferter. Part of this land had been granted by State to sd Reagon and part granted to William Nelson and bought by sd Reagon. July 3, 1801. M. Harden, James Campbell, John Whitten.

Book A, page 39. Peter Martin to John Morehead Esq. for $140 100 A on Horse Pasture Cr of Dan R adj Parke Farley. May 26, 1801. Jonathan Noble, John Stephens.

Book A, page 40. Peter Martin to John Morehead Esq. for 60 pds 50 A on both sides Burchfields fork of Wolf Island Cr. May 26, 1801. Jonathan Noble, John Stephens.

Book A, page 43. (Pages 41 & 42 missing and most of this document) "that at expiration of ...seven yrs James Taylor... shall be allowed... compensation for building improvements, etc. Signed John Dunbar, James Taylor. Wits: Peter Teary, John Louis Taylor.

Book A, page 43. State of N. C. to John Majors 14 A on Blewes Cr. Dec. 30, 1790.

Book A, page 44. State of N. C. to William Patterson 238 A on both sides Londons Cr of Wolf Island Cr adj Mark London, William Stubblefield. Nov. 8, 1784.

Book A, page 45. State of N. C. to John McCubbin 200 A on Burchfield fork of Wolf Island Cr adj Joseph Patterson, Mark London. Oct. 14, 1783.

Book A, page 46. Edward Hunter of Lincoln Co to John Menzies for 500 pds 609 A on Dan R adj McCain's Line, John Leak. Land granted by Granville to Robert Jones Jr. and sold to sd Hunter. May 23, 1786. R. Martin, James Martin, John McNary, Thomas Henderson.

Book A, page 48. State of N. C. to Charles Toney 150 A on Town Cr adj Norrisses line. Oct. 14, 1783.

Book A, page 49. State of N. C. to Michael Trolliner 100 A on Jacobs Cr adj Alexander Brown, Hays corner, Martin's line, crossing Rocky fork of Jacobs Cr. Oct. 8, 1783.

Book A, page 50. State of N. C. to Adam Holker for 300 A on both sides of Troublesome Cr adj Hugh Harkins. Aug. 8, 1786.

Book A, page 51. State of N. C. to Nathaniel Linder 150 A on Gr Rockhouse Cr adj Matthews Mount, Thomas King. May 16, 1787.

Book A, page 52. State of N. C. to Joseph Patterson 200 A on both sides Burchfields fork of Wolk Island Cr adj John McCubbin, _____ Parker. Nov. 18, 1784.

Book A, page 53. State of N. C. to Charles Harris 150 A on Wolf Island Cr. adj Joseph Burton. Oct. 14, 1783.

Book A, page 54. State of N. C. to Elmore Walker 200 A on both sides Majas Cr. May 16, 1787.

Book A, page 55. State of N. C. to William Jones 500 A on both sides Big Troublesome Cr adj Widdow Dickson, William Lemonds, John O. Daniel. Oct. 22, 1782.

Book A, page 56. State of N. C. to Robert Boak 200 A between the two Troublesome Crs. May 16, 1787.

Book A, page 57. State of N. C. to William Plumley 520 A on Piney fork of Gr. Troublesome Cr. Nov. 8, 1784.

Book A, page 58. State of N. C. to Jesse Browden 500 A on head of Rocky Br and head of Little Troublesome Cr adj Hugh Harkins, Adam Heather, Benjamin Grainger, Andrew Martin. Nov. 8, 1784.

Book A, page 59. State of N. C. to Robert Martin 150 A on both sides SW fork of Jacobs Cr adj Robert Nelson, James Hays. Nov. 8, 1784.

Book A, page 60. State of N. C. to William Plumber 600 A on both sides Piney Cr adj John Mackey. May 16, 1787.

Book A, page 61. State of N. C. to Charles Baker 15 A on Brushy fork of Piney Cr adj Adam Walker. Nov. 8, 1784.

Book A, page 62. State of N. C. to John Allen 640 A on Little Troublesome Cr adj Harris line, John Hodge. June 27, 1787.

Book A, page 63. State of N. C. to Charles Baker 150 A on Brushy fork of Piney Cr adj Robert Small, Adam Walker. Nov. 9, 1784.

Book A, page 64. State of N. C. to Patrick Hayes 100 A on both sides Upper Hogans Cr adj John Burn. Nov. 8, 1784.

Book A, page 65. State of N. C. to Gideon Johnston 125 A on Moses Cr of Dan R adj own land. Oct. 22, 1782.

Book A, page 66. State of N. C. to Benjamin Bowen 639 A on W Fork of upper Hogans Cr. adj Thomas Bowin. Oct. 22, 1782.

Book A, page 67. Thomas Rafferty to John Morehead for $730½ 150 A on Wolf Island Cr adj William Bethell, Leven Mitchell, Isaac Cantrell. Sept. 5, 1801. William Raffety, John Raffety.

Book A, page 68. Archelaus Hughes of Henry Co., Va. to John Wimbish of Pittsylvania Co., Va. for 20 sh. Va. currency 630 A on both sides Beaver Island Cr, being same land bought from Thomas Neal, Sarah Neal and Judith Neal Aug. 5, 1772 and recorded in Guilford.. Aug. 26, 1784. Thomas Jemison, Lemuel Smith, Henry Scales, Peter Perkins, Watson Gentry, William Dalton, William Martin.

Book A, page 70. William Plumber to Speedwell Congregation 1 A for 5 sh, being part of 520 A grant to William Plumber on S side of Piney Cr adj Peter Perkins. April 7, 1786. John Steward, William Langford, George Lemond.

Book A, page 71. Zaza Brasher to Jesse Brasher, his son, for 100 pds 42 A in fork of Jacobs Cr adj Sampson Knight, Jas Hays, Widdow Oliver. 1801. Jesse Brasher.

Book A, page 72. Martha Caruthers of Guilford Co. to Jacob Whitworth Sr. of Guilford for 200 pds 125 A on Jacobs Cr. Dec. 15, 1785. George Oliver, Zaza Brasher, Phillip Gates.

Book A, page 73. John Hallums & wife Elizabeth to Isaac Kello for 80 pds 100 A on N side of Little Troublesome Cr. Feb. 10, 1786. A. Philips, Isaac Kello, Samuel Griffith.

Book A, page 76. Benjamin Silman to William Proctor a sum 250 A on Little Rockhouse Cr. adj Martin line, Galloway line, Town Road. Dec. 10, 1785. John Morton, William Young, James Cotton.

Book A, page 77. Joseph Reid to Hugh Reid for 100 pds 100 A between the Lickfork and Pruets fork of Hogans Cr. adj Gordon Smith, John Martin. Nov. 23, 1801. Benjamin Settle, Thomas North.

Book A, page 78. John Morton to Thomas Barnard for 200 pds 180 A on Little Rockhouse Cr. Oct. 31, 1785. George Peay, Richard Covington, John Peay.

Book A, page 79. Jonathan Norton of Guilford Co. to William Fields for 45 pds 100 A on br of Lickfork of Buffalo Island Cr. Dec. 23, 1785. Turbefield Barnes, John Bradley.

Book A, page 81. Samuel Dalton Senr to David Dalton for 50 pds 330 A on N side of Mayo R adj Drury Smith, Nimiah Vernon and crossing Pap Paw Cr & Brushy fork. Nov. 22, 1785. Daniel Grogan, John Joyce, Frances Grogan, Zachariah Smith.

Book A, page 84. James Gill & wife Mary to Edward Scott for 110 pds 200 A on Hogans Cr. adj Samuel Watt, Charles Dean, Wall's line, being part of a grant to William Long in 1783. Feb. 20, 1786. Mary Dailey, Catherine Gill, William Bethell.

Book A, page 86. Isaac Wright to Benjamin Stone for 100 pds 162 A on N side Troublesome Cr. Aug. 11, 1787. Asa Brasher, Charles Bruce.

Book A, page 88. John Duncan to Elijah Joyce for 50 pds 200 A on Shepherds Cr adj Elijah Joyce, Isaac Vernon, John Joyce. Aug. 13, 1786. Enos Hooper, Andrew Joyce, John Barnes.

Book A, page 90. Martha Caruthers to Phillip Gates for 125 pds 120 A on Brushey fork of Jacobs Cr. Dec. 12, 1785. George Oliver, Zaza Brasher, Jacob Whitworth.

Book A, page 92. Peter Perkins to Reace Price for 25 pds Va. currency 165 A adj John Leak, Farley line, John Tackett. Nov. 10, 1785.

Book A, page 94. John Smith to William Russell for 50 pds 158 A on both sides Wolf Island Cr adj Hugh Challes. Dec. 28, 1785. A. Phillips, Aaron Cantrell.

Book A, page 96. James Harrison to John Gibson for 50 pds Proclamation money 100 A in Middle fork of Buffalo Island Cr. adj Joseph Odell, being part of a grant to Joseph Odell Mar. 1, 1779. Aug. 11, 1786. J. Holderness, James Gallaway, Henry Scales.

Book A, page 98. John Smith to William Russell for 10 pds 24 A
on Wolf Island Cr. being part of grant to Smith from Granville
in 1760. Dec. 28, 1785. A. Phillips, Aaron Cantrell.

Book A, page 99. Gideon Johnston to William Johnston for 50 pds
240 A on both sides Moses Cr adj Gideon Johnston, Joab Walker,
William Aston.

Book A, page 102. James Jones to William Bethell for 100 pds
50 A on N side Hogans Cr adj Charles Dean, being part of tract
deeded to Benjamin Ellis from Sam'l Parker. Aug. 29, 1786.
Jeremiah Norris, Stephen Childres.

Book A, page 104. John Cummins of Surry Co. to Sarah Kirkpatrick
for 100 pds 400 A near head springs of Findleys Br adj Samuel
Findley, Hugh Kirkpatrick. Mar. 6, 1786.

Book A, page 106. Turbefield Barnes to Elisha Joyce for 12 pds
53 A on both sides Mountain Run of Mayo R adj Joyce's own land.
Aug. 29, 1786. John Fields, George Peay, Nehemiah Vernon.

Book A, page 108. Adam Holker to John Haines for 100 pds 300 A
on both sides Little Troublesome adj Hugh Harkins.

Book A, page 110. James Sanders to Alexander McClaran for 40
pds 25 A on E side Gr Rockhouse Cr., part of grant from Granville to James Simms 1760, later sold to William Hill. Aug. 30,
1786. George Tankersley, James Hayes, Abner Johnson.

Book A, page 112. John Glenn to William Glenn for 50 pds 150 A
on both sides Reed Cr of Dan R adj James Walker. May 20, 1786.
Joshua Smith, Phomas Paren, Abraham Glenn.

Book A, page 114. Elijah Joyce to Elisha Joyce for 200 pds 200
A on both sides the Mountain Run adj his fathers line, Joshua
Smith, Mary Fields. Aug. 29, 1786. John Whitworth, Jesse
Lyes (?), Jarrette Patterson.

Book A, page 116. William James of Lawrence Co., S. C. grants
Power of Attorney to Sharrod Brook in settlement with bros.
Isaac James, Abraham James, Jacob James and mother Susanna James
in estate of father Abraham James decd. Oct. 24, 1786. John
Leak, George Vandlandingham.

Book A, page 117. Zachariah Standley of Louisa Co., Va. grants
Power of Atty. to friend Samuel Henderson of Guilford to convey
by deed to Henry Hardin 200 A on Beaver Island Cr adj James
Scales, Thomas S. Hill, Elizabeth Conner, Nelley Garner. May
10, 1783. Isaac Whitworth.

Book A, page 118. Isaac James of Lawrence Co., S. C. grants
Power of Atty to Nathaniel Harris in settlement with bros
William James, Abraham James, Jacob James and mother Susanna
James of est. of father Abraham James dec'd. Oct. 18, 1786.
Archer Murphrey, Jesse Harris.

Book A, page 119. Thomas Conner - Gift Deed to sons John &
William Conner of "my goods and Chattells, dwelling house, all

my lands, etc." Jan. 10, 1786. Daniel Draytor, Robert Bethell.

Book A, page 120. Thomas Holgin to Moses Yell for 150 pds 113 A on both sides Gr Troublesome Cr. adj James McNealy, part of grant to Simon Dunn Mar. 1, 178_. Nov. 15, 1786. A. Phillips, Thomas Gray, James McNealy.

Book A, page 121. William Walker Sr. and wife Mary to Peter O'Neal for 30 pds 61 A on Country line Cr. adj Jeremiah Poston, Walker's own land. July 30, 1786. John Hevo or Hero, Stephen Williamson, James Appleton, James Williams.

Book A, page 123. Zachariah Standley of Louisa Co., Va. to Henry Hardin for 100 pds 200 A on both sides N & S forks Beaver Island Cr., being part of grant from Granville to Joseph Scales dec'd. Aug. 29, 1786. Isham Reigs, Hehemiah Vernon.

Book A, page 125. William Barnes to John Phillips for 193 pds pure money 342 A on both sides Mountain Run of Mayo adj Mary Fields, John Fields, Joshua Smith, Richard Vernon. Nov. 28, 1786. James Scales, John Hunter.

Book A, page 127. Champ Gilson to Robert Means for 10 pds 50 A on both sides Hiccory Cr of Mayo R. 1786. Joshua Smith, Joseph Scales.

Book A, page 129. Archibald Lytel of Orange Co. to Peter Perkins for 1,000 pds 640 A on both sides Troublesome Cr and known as the Ironworks tract, adj Robert Small, James McClendale, William Tramill. May 13, 1786. Lemuel Smith, William Astin, Joseph Clendenin.

Book A, page 131. Edmund Brewer & wife Sarah to Joseph Scales for 50 pds Va. money 324 A on N side Dan R adj Thomas Joyce. Aug. 9, 1786.

Book A, page 133. William Plumber to Peter Perkins for 86 pds 96 A on S side of Piney Creek adj John Mabery, Perkins line. Apr. 7, 1786. Lemuel Smith, William Langford, Hugh Lynch.

Book A, page 135. Charles Harris to John Scogin for 200 pds 550 A on both sides Wolf Island Cr adj Joseph Burton, Reubin Dickson, Isaac Cantrel. Dec. 20, 1784. William Steward, John Hussy or Hurry.

Book A, page 137. James Reagon to William Colwell for 100 pds 120 A on both sides Hogans Cr adj William Tronett. Aug. 26, 1786. John Pound, Sherwood Toney.

Book A, page 139. Turbefield Barnes to Robert Donald and Company, merchants in Petersburg, Va., for 400 pds Va. money 150 A bought of Jesse Thomas adj James Gallaway and Richard Sharp; 350 A bought of William Lewis adj James Gallaway, Richard Sharp, James Holderness; 410 A bought of Arron Gowin adj Thomas Henderson and Matrimony and Pau Pau Crs. and the Va. line; 100 A bought of Jonathan Norton adj Allen Dodd, George Colston. Oct. 21, 1786. Robert Galloway, John Menzies, Charles Gallaway, James Campbell.

Book A, page 142. Reubin Cook to Edward Daniel for 10 pds 600 A on Matrimony Cr adj Samuel Gales, John Roach, Henry Grogan,

the Va. line. Joshua Smith, Alexander McClaran, John Reagon.
Mar. 5, 1784.

Book A, page 144. Watson Gentry to Henry Hardin for 100 pds 50
A adj Sarah Jones, Isham Rice, Benjamin Cook. Mar. 20, 1786.
Benjamin Cook, Mark Hardin.

Book A, page 146. Alse Siers (her mark) to Sarah Powell for 50
pds Va. money 80 A on Mayo R adj Elisha Joyce, Mary Fields,
Joshua Smith. Jan. 16, 1784. Joshua Smith, Jesse Siers, Enuch
Siers.

Book A, page 149. Robert Vernon to William Barnes for 130 pds
342 A on both sides Mountain Run of Mayo R adj Mary Fields, John
Fields, Joshua Smith. Jan. 27, 1785. James Vernon, Nelley
Vernon.

Book A, page 152. Joseph Cunningham to John Jones for 50 pds
110 A on head waters of Brushey fork of Gr Rockhouse Cr. Feb.
24, 1787. A. Phillips, John Conner, John Cunningham.

Book A, page 154. Thomas Sparks to Joseph McClain for 5 pds 50
A of a grant to Sparks Mar. 1, 1780 on both sides Dixes Ferry
Road on Lickfork of Hogans Cr adj William Bethell. 1786.
Nathaniel Linders, John Odell, William Bethell, Thomas Chance,
Thomas McClain, Sarah Washband.

Book A, page 156. James Caruthers to John Chadwell for 100 pds
400 A on head waters of Brushey fork of Jacobs Cr adj Martha
Caruthers, Phillip Gates. Jan. 25, 1787. William W. Allen,
James Regan.

Book A, page 158. James Leak to Reece Price for 50 pds 100 A
adj Leak's land on Matrimony Cr. Nov. 28, 1786. Joshua Smith,
John Leak, Philip Ross.

Book A, page 160. Joseph Cunningham to John Cunningham Jr. for
50 pds 130 A of grant for 500 A on Nov. 8, 1780 on S side of
Jacobs Cr adj Thomas King, John Jones. Feb. 24, 1787. John
Connor, William Cunningham.

Book A, page 161. Samuel Bethell & wife Mary to Thomas Mullen
for 50 pds 65 A on Lickfork of Hogans Cr, being part of land
bought of Richard Leigh, originally granted to John Mullin.
Feb. 9, 1787. William McCollum, William Smith, William Bethell.

Book A, page 163. Watson Gentry to Sarah Gentry for 10 pds 100
A on Shepherds Cr of Mayo R. Feb. 27, 1786.

Book A, page 165. Joseph Payne & wife Martha to James Walker
for 20 pds 92 A on Jiles Cr. adj Walker's line, William Roberson.
Feb. 24, 1787. Peter Oneal, James Higgins.

Book A, page 167. Joseph Cloud of Greenbices Co. on western
waters of N. C. to Lyrus Lightfoot Roberts for 500 pds 150 A
on S side of Dan R, orig. granted to Robert Jones by Granville,
sold to James Watkins in Granville Co. and sold to Joseph Cloud
in Rowan Co. Feb. 7, 1787. William Cloud, Benjamin Cloud.

Book A, page 169. Abraham James, Jacob James and Sherod Brock,

Atty for William James and Nathaniel Harris, Atty. for Isaac
James, to Henry Grogan for 45 pds land on both sides Matrimony
Cr adj Grogan land. Jan. 9, 1787. Ezekiel Callahan, Jesse
Harris.

Book A, page 171. William Stepts of Fairfax Co., Va. to Ancel
Fields for 20 pds 200 A on Pappaw Cr of Mayo R. Feb. 3, 1786.
Alexander Sall, Thomas Robson.

Book A, page 174. Thomas McCullough to John Doneky for 15 pds
50 A on Hogans Cr adj John Hodges. Feb. 28, 1787. A. Philips,
Nathaniel Lanier.

Book A, page 176. Abraham James, Jacob James, Sherod Brock Atty.
for William James and Nathaniel Harris Atty. for Isaac James to
Henry Grogan for 45 pds land on Matrimony Cr of Dan R. Jan. 9,
1787. Ezekiel Callahan, Jesse Harris.

Book A, page 179. Michael Henderson of Surry Co. to George
Hamblin for 100 pds 165 A on W fork of Hogans Cr. Oct. 4, 1786.
William Williams, James Reagon, Joseph Hamblin.

Book A, page 181. Benjamin Gates to Robert Warren for 45 pds
100 A on Sharps Cr. adj Thomas Henderson, Gates, Vernon. Feb.
4, 1786. Joshua Smith, William Wright, Leonard Barker.

Book A, page 183. Joseph Cunningham to William Cunningham for
50 pds 500 A. Feb. 24, 1787. A. Phillips, John Conner, John
Jones.

Book A, page 185. John Joyce to James Belton for 40 pds 200 A
on both sides Fish Pot Cr of Mayo R adj Richard Cardwell,
Blacksmith John Joyce. Feb. 2, 1787. Joshua Smith, Richard
Bondurant, Andrew Joyce.

Book A, page 188. William Lankston Lewis to Mathew Sims for 150
pds 300 A on Lickfork of Buffalo Island Cr, being granted to
Lewis 1783. May 17, 1786. John Hill, James Rhodes.

Book A, page 190. John Strong to James Strong 136 A on each
side Buffalo Island Cr. adj Daniel Wilson. Feb. 26, 1787. Tho.
M_____, George Peay Jr.

Book A, page 191. John McKibben & wife Margaret to John Hamil-
ton of Guilford Co. for 150 pds 450 A on Bosses Cr. adj William
Matear, John Haynes. Mar. 17, 1787. John Hunter, Thomas
Searcy.

Book A, page 193. State of N. C. to John Burton of Guilford Co.
250 A on Wolf Island Cr. adj Allen Williams, Luke Barnard,
Jacob Barnard. May 16, 1780.

Book A, page 194. Henry Hays & wife Nancy to Joseph Griffin for
100 pds 300 A on Lickfork of Hogans Cr adj John Baker. Feb. 10,
1787. William Cockrell, Jurat, David Reid.

Book A, page 196. Thomas Holgin to James Minealy for 200 pds
87 A on Gr Troublesome Cr adj Moses Yell, part of grant dated
Mar. 4, 1780 to Holgin. Nov. 15, 1786. Moses Yell, Thomas Gray.

Book A, page 198. Isaac White of Washington Co. to Joshua Pruitt for 53 pds 91 A on Lickfork of Hogans Cr adj the Moravian line, being part of grant of 640 A to White. Dec. 22, 1786. Hugh Reed, Samuel Pruitt, John McCollum, Jurat.

Book A, page 199. James Wright to William Mateer for certain sum 20 A adj Christopher Vandergriph. Feb. 27, 1787.

Book A, page 201. Jonathon Norton to George Colson for 12 pds 100 A on Lickfork of Buffalo Island Cr adj William Thomas. Oct. 27, 1785. Joshua Smith, Allen Dodd, James Rhodes, Jurat.

Book A, page 203. Job Loftis to James Powell for 50 pds 104 A on Lickfork of Hogans Cr adj John Mount, William Hickman. Feb. 20, 1787. William Hickman, Jurat, Thaddeus Owen, William Hubbert.

Book A, page 205. Adam Tate as heir at law, son of Joseph Tate dec'd, to John Joyce for 426.13.4, 336 A on both sides Beaver Island Cr adj James Hunter's old line, John Davis. May 20, 1786. James Martin, James Leak.

Book A, page 207. James Tomlinson to John Tomlinson for 40 pds 100 A adj Thomas Williams, Hickman, Widdow Mullins. April 11, 1786. Eli Lane, John Tomlinson.

Book A, page 209. Thomas Rice of Granville Co. to Edward Mulloy of Guilford Co. 150 A on Haw R and Troublesome Cr adj William Kewes, Hezekiah Roads. Nov. 7, 1786. Robert Burton, James Sallerabet (?), Jas. Mulloy.

Book A, page 211. Thomas Moor to James Mulloy for 40 pds 47 A on SE fork of Richland Cr. Jan. 26, 1787. A. Phillips, George Lemond, John Rhodes.

Book A, page 213. Joel Gibson to William Mills of Henry Co., Va. for 60 pds 200 A on E side of Mayo River adj William Kellam. Oct. 10, 1786. Joshua Smith, Turbefield Barnes, Richard Bonduvans.

Book A, page 215. Isaac Lowe & wife Catherine to John Edmondson for 40 pds 100 A on Little Troublesome Cr adj John Hallum, John Lewis, being part of grant to Joseph Chapman 1783. Dec. 20, 1786. Isaac Kello, John Hallum, Isaac Kello.

Book A, page 219. Richard Leigh to Samuel Bethell for 100 pds 100 A on Lickfork of Hogans Cr adj John Mullin. Jan. 24, 1787. Sampson Bethell, William Bethell.

Book A, page 221. Joseph Pain Johnson to John Hill for 5 pds 137 A on Buffalo Cr of Dan R adj William Hill. 1786. James Hill, John Hill, Matthew Sims, Jurat.

Book A, page 223. Thaddeus Owen to James Tomlinson for 40 pds 100 A adj Thomas Williams, Widdow Mullin, Burton. Jan. 11, 1786. Job Loftis, John Conn. (The name Owen is guesswork. It is spelled with an O followed by 4 crooked s-looking letters.)

Book A, page 226. Thomas Henderson to John Cunningham for 10 pds 38 A on N side Troublesome Cr. Nov. 30, 1786.

Book A, page 227. Abraham Fielkerson of Caswell Co. to William Barksdale of Dunwoody Co., Va. 100 pds for 141 A on Lickfork of Hogans Cr. Apr. 17, 1786. Thomas Chambers, Pemberton Burch.

Book A, page 229. William Brown to Richard Marr 100 pds for 500 A on Burchfields Cr of Wolf Island Cr adj Benjamin Parrott, a tract entered by Joshua Brown 1782. Jan. 7, 1786. Thomas Allen, Reubin Tyler, David Burton.

Book A, page 231. Abraham Benton & wife Sarah to Abner Raeley for 20 pds 50 A on Lickfork of Hogans Cr adj Job Loftis, William Chambers, part of grant in 1784 to Benton. May 10, 1786. William Bethell, Fanne Cham_r., Rebechah Chane.

Book A, page 234. John Mattock & wife Sarah to Jeremiah Thacker for 30 pds 200 A on Pruitts Br of Hogans Cr adj Samuel Watts, Josiah Sithes, Joseph Garner, Nathaniel Williams. May 20, 1786. Peter O'Neal, William Clark.

Book A, page 236. Archebald Yarbrough to Wyatt Stubblefield of Caswell Co. for 21 pds Va. money 21 A on both sides County line of Caswell and Rockingham on br of Hogans Cr. Apr. 27, 1786. Richard Beasley, John Duncan, William Brown.

Book A, page 238. Abraham Benton to William Barksdale of Va. for 100 pds 178½ A on Lickfork of Hogans Cr adj Barksdale. Mar. 24, 1786. Abraham Fielkerson, Thomas Chambers, William Mount.

Book A, page 240. John Morton to Peter Perkins for 1,200 pds 300 A on SE side Dan R adj John Watkins. Mar. 25, 1786. Nathaniel Scales, Jeremiah Nance, Geo. Peay.

Book A, page 242. James Roberts to Naman Roberts for 5 pds 400 A on S side Dan R adj John Morton, Peter Perkins, James Roberts. Feb. 3, 1786. Phillip Rose, Dorcas Roberts, Ezra Roberts.

Book A, page 243. Zachariah Standley of Louisa Co., Va. to William Johnson Power of Atty to sell to Alexander McClaran 100 A on Hogans Cr. May 12, 1785. Gideon Johnson, Peter Johnson, Isaac Whitworth.

Book A, page 244. James Roberts to Naman Roberts for 5 pds 134 A on Clouds Cr of Dan R adj James Roberts, George Carter. Feb. 3, 1786. Phillip Rose, Ezra Roberts.

Book A, page 246. Zachariah Standley of Louisa Co., Va. to John Oliver for 53 pds 100 A on Hogans Cr on S side of Dan R. May 23, 1786. John Hunter Jr.

Book A, page 247. James Watkins Jr. (son of Beverly Watkins of Surry Co.) to Elizabeth Roberts for 25 pds 170 A on N side Dan R adj Naman Roberts, Rose, being land granted by Granville to Robert Jones thence to James Watkins Sr. thence to his son Beverley Watkins and thence to his son James Watkins. Mar. 4, 1786. Darby Callahan, Philip Wilson, David Davis.

Book A, page 250. John May to Sneed Strong for 88 pds 50 A on

Schoolhouse Br of Dan R adj sd May's line, John Simmons, Robert's line. 1786.

Book A, page 251. Manlove Torrant to William Bethell for 50 pds 100 A on Hogans Cr adj William Wibon, Richard Ellis, Joseph Mc-Clain, James Horsford. May 10, 1786. John Orineal, William McCollum, Isaac McCollum. Signed by Samuel Bethell Atty for M. Torrant.

Book A, page 253. William Plumley to Andrew Martin Sr. for 100 pds 223 A on Piney Cr adj William Plumley and wife Phebe Plumley. Apr. 1, 1786. Soloman Webster, Walter Martin.

Book A, page 254. James Horsford to William Bethell for 50 pds 50 A on S side of Chambers Mill Road adj Elmore's line, being land granted to Horsford. May 20, 1786. John Horsford, Samuel Bethell.

Book A, page 256. Jesse Braughton of Nash Co. to Peter Perkins for 50 pds 500 A on Little Troublesome Cr adj Hugh Harkins, John Haines, Benjamin Granger, William Plumley. May 1, 1786. Nath. Lawson, Jacob Cockrell.

Book A, page 257. Job Loftis to William Barksdale of Dunwooda Co., Va. for 200 pds 229 A on Lickfork of Hogans Cr adj William Hickman. Mar. 24, 1786. William Hickman, Thomas Chambers, Henry Hays.

Book A, page 259. Jacob Caton of Henry Co., Va. to John Hampton for 30 pds 240 A on N side Dan R and White Stone Cr adj John Simons, John May. May 23, 1786. Gideon Johnson Sr., Allen Walker, Mark Hardin Sr.

Book A, page 261. Jeremiah Thacker to William Cockrill for 600 pds 150 A on Lickfork of Hogans Cr adj William Chambers, Mary Fielkerson. May 6, 1786. John Odineal, Joseph McClain, William Bethell.

Book A, page 263. Constant Perkins and Charles Galloway grant Power of Atty to James Jordon and Richard Harrison, Justices of the Peace in Spartanburg, S. C. to gain signature from Sarah Mitchell of S. C. to relinquish her Dower of land in Rockingham already deeded to sd Perkins and Galloway, 200 A on E side of Rockhouse Cr by Charles Mitchell and wife Sarah. Nov. 28, 1787.

Book A, page 264. James Jordan, JP and Richard Harrison, JP of Spartanburg, S. C. to County Court of Rockingham Co., N. C. statement that Sarah Mitchell voluntarily and on her own free will relinquishes her right to aforesaid described lands which her husband Charles Mitchell sold to Constant Perkins and Charles Galloway. Dec. 28, 1787.

Book A, page 265. State of N. C. to Thomas Hopper 100 A on Big br of Matrimony Cr adj Hopper's own line, Joshua Hopper. May 16, 1787.

Book A, page 266. State of N. C. to William Marter 50 A on Haw R adj his land, John McKibbon, Andrew Martin. May 16, 1787.

Book A, page 268. State of N. C. to Thomas Holgan 32 A between the two Troublesomes adj Andrew Boyd. May 16, 1787.

Book A, page 269.   State of N.C. to William Weaben 108 A on Lickfork of Hogans Cr adj James Horsford, Allen land. Oct. 14, 1783.

Book A, page 270.   State of N.C. to Robert Martin 290 A on fork
of Piney Cr adj William Plumblie, Robert Borch, A. Martin, Jesse
Braughton. May 16, 1787.

Book A, page 271.   State of N.C. to John Mount 200 A on Lickfork
of Hogans Cr adj Henry Dickson, John Hancock, John Smith. May
16, 1787.

Book A, page 272.   State of N.C. to Stephen Sephew 129 A on little
Rockhouse Cr adj William Elliott, Benjamin Silman, Charles Galloway, Mary Elliott. Nov. 8, 1784.

Book A, page 274.   State of N.C. to Thomas Williams 180 A on
N fork of Hogans Cr adj George Mitchell, David Vaughn, James
Hays, Benton land. Nov. 8, 1785.

Book A, page 275.   State of N.C. to Archibald Lytle for 140 A
on both sides Troublesome Cr adj James McCleland, William Trammill. Jan. 5, 1785.

Book A, page 277.   State of N.C. to William Tranum 300 A on Londons Cr of Wolf Island Cr adj Nicholas McCubbin. May 16, 1787.

Book A, page 279.   State of N.C. to Christopher Kobler 200 A on
Matrimony Cr adj Kobler's own land, Va. line, Nathaniel Harris.
May 8, 1784.

Book A, page 280.   State of N.C. to George Roland in trust for
John & Thomas Wilson, orphans, 400 A on Hogans Cr on br called
Rentsfork adj Settle land. May 16, 1787.

Book A, page 282.   State of N.C. to Frederich Cobler 50 A on both
sides Matrimony Cr adj own line, Henry Grogan, Christopher Cobler. May 16, 1787.

Book A, page 284.   State of N.C. to Simon Dunn 200 A on both
sides Gr. Troublesome Cr. March 1, 1780.

Book A, page 285.   State of N.C. to Thomas Holgan 200 A on N
side Big Troublesome Cr adj Mateers line, Sprout's line. May
16, 1787.

Book A, page 286.   Henry Scales to Charles Galloway for 100 pds
80 A on both sides Dan R and Smith River at fork, adj Colonel
Farley, Charles Galloway, Nathaniel Scales. May 23, 1787.
James Holderness, Nathaniel Scales, James Campbell.

Book A, page 289.   James Vernon & wife Elinor to Charles Gallo-
way & Company for 350 pds Va. money 313 A on S side Mayo R adj
William Beaver, Leonard Barker, Richard Vernon, Robert Axton.
March 12, 1787.   Geo. Peay, Joshua Smith, John Joyce.

Book A, page 292.   Elinor Vernon, wife of James Vernon, relinquishes her right of Dower for above property to be sold. May
29, 1787.   Geo. Peay, J.P., Joshua Smith, J.P.

Book A, page 292.   Charles Mitchell to Constant Perkins and
Charles Galloway for 225 pds Va. currency 100 A on Rocky Br of

12

Rockhouse Cr adj Mitchell's own land. Apr. 26, 1787. J. Holderness, James Pratt, Sr., James Campbell, Robert Galloway.

Book A, page 295. Charles Mitchell to Constant Perkins and Charles Galloway for 225 pds 100 A on Bear Swamp Br of Big Rockhouse Cr adj Mitchell's own land, Henderson land. April 26, 1787. J. Holderness, James Campbell, Ro. Galloway, James Pratt Sr.

Book A, page 297. Ezekiel Cavender and Guy Vermilion for 58 pds 8 sh 150 A on both sides Little fork of Wolf Island Cr adj Joseph Curry, Nathaniel Harrison, Banister's line, John Odineal. Sept. 9, 1786. A. Phillips, William Jones, Isham Lanier.

Book A, page 299. Joseph Odell to John Gibson for 40 pds 30 A on middle fork of Buffalo Island Cr adj Gibson's land, being part of grant dated Mar. 1, 1779 to Odell. May 24, 1787. Henry Scales, Thomas Galloway, Jurat.

Book A, page 301. Isham Lanier to John Bankson for 60 pds 123 A on Big Troublesome Cr adj John Fabicomer, Henry Brewer, being part of grant to John Faboner in 1782. Sept. 21, 1785. A. Phillips, Cynthia Phillips, Stephen Brown.

Book A, page 303. Charles Harris to William Steward Moberly for 50 pds 100 A on Wolf Island Cr adj Joseph Burton. Dec. 20, 1784. John Scogin, John Harris.

Book A, page 305. Gift Deed of David Vaun & wife Sarah to son-in-law, Thomas Adams and our dau. Anny Adams, his wife 126 A on Pruitts fork of Hogans Cr including plantation on which we now live, adj James Hays. Mar. 12, 1787. Robert Mitchell, Henry Hayes.

Book A, page 306. Thomas Henderson, Clerk of Court, grants Power of Atty to George Peay and Joshua Smith to confirm that Elinor Vernon, wife of James Vernon makes free consent to deed to Charles Galloway & Company, said Elinor Vernon being an inhabitant of our State and so old and infirm that she cannot travel to our sd Court to be held fourth Monday of Feb. 1787.

Book A, page 308. James Pratt to William Pratt of Caswell Co. for 20 pds Va. money 50 A on Sharps Cr adj James Holderness. Dec. 27, 1786. Wm. L. Lewis, Richard Pratt.

Book A, page 310. John Boggs & wife of Linkhorn Co. to John Hodge for 120 pds 200 A on N side Haw River adj Dilworth, Boyd, being that tract on which John Boggs & wife Jane formerly lived. May 4, 1787. Walter Martin, James Walker, Alexander Walker.

Book A, page 312. Gift Deed of David Vaughan & wife Sarah to son-in-law George Thomas and our dau Senia Thomas, his wife, 66 A on Pruetts fork of Hogans Cr adj Thomas Adams. Mar. 12, 1787. Robert Mitchell, Saul Read, William Loftis.

Book A, page 313. John Abbott to Thomas Pound for 60 pds 100 A on Wolf Island Cr adj John McCarril, Jarratt Brannon, being part of land granted Luke Bernard in 1782. May 27, 1787. Sherwood Toney, James Colton, Robert Brown.

Book A, page 315. John Scoggin to Charles Cantrell and Robert Cantrell for 81 pds part of 500 A granted to Charles Harris Oct. 2, 1782 on both sides Wolf Island Cr. adj Edward Williams. Sept. 21, 1786. A. Phillips, Jacob _____ (torn).

Book A, page 317. Hezekiah Rhodes & wife Alamenter to Stephen Mitchell for 320 pds 640 A on Haw R and Troublesome Cr. adj James Martin, being land granted to Rhodes Mar. 1, 1779. (Rest of deed torn.) June 1786.

Book A, page 319. John Nance to Daniel Sillevan of Henry Co., Va. for 50 pds 100 A on S fork of Stewards Cr adj Virginia line. May 28, 1787.

BOOK B

Book B, page 3. (First 2 pages missing). Abraham Benton & wife Sarah to Abner Railey for 20 pds 50 A on Lickfork of Hogans Cr adj Job Loftis, William Chambers. May 10, 1786. William Bethell, Fanne Chanie, Rebekah Chanie.

Book B, page 4. Abraham Benton to William Barksdale of Va. for 100 pds 178½ A on Lickfork of Hogans Cr adj Barksdales own land. Mar. 24, 1786. Abraham Fulknon, Thomas Chambers, William Mount.

Book B, page 5. Job Loftis to William Barksdale of Dunwoodie Co., Va. for 200 pds 229 A on Lickfork of Hogans Cr adj Moravin land, William Hickman. Mar. 24, 1786. Abraham Fulknon, Thomas Chambers, Henry Hays, William Mount.

Book B, page 6. James Watkins Jr. (son of Beverley Watkins) to Elizabeth Roberts for 25 pds 170 A on N side of Dan R adj Namon Roberts, Rose land. Mar. 10, 1786. Darby Calahan, Philip Wilson, David Davis.

Book B, page 7. James Roberts to Naaman Roberts for 5 pds 400 A on S side Dan R adj John Morton, Peter Perkins, James Roberts. Feb. 3, 1786. Philip Rose, Dorcas Roberts, Ezra Roberts.

Book B, page 8. John Allen Sr. to Joseph McCullock for 160 pds 343 A on Little Troublesome Cr and Hogans Cr adj Coleson's line, John Hodge, Thomas Conners. Sept. 3, 1787. John Herrin, William Philips.

Book B, page 9. James Coleman of Halifax Co., Va. to James Galloway for 250 pds 200 A on S side Dan R. May 20, 1788. Presley Carter, Thomas Word, George Carter.

Book B, page 10. Thomas Reeves, Jesse Reeves and James Reeves, Heirs of Malachiah Reeves dec'd to Nathaniel Tatum for 176 pds 352 A on both sides Haw R adj John Rhodes, Peter Perkins, Esq., William Conners. May 28, 1788. Jas. Mulloy, John Rhodes, William Howlet.

Book B, page 12. David Peoples & wife Elizabeth of Guilford Co. to Ralph Shaw of Guilford Co. for 75 pds 150 A on Jacobs Cr adj Peter Mitchell. May 24, 1788.

Book B, page 13. Isham Rice & wife Frances to Peter Hairston of Surry Co. for 100 pds 197 A on W side Mayo R. Feb. 21, 1788. J. W. Bostick, John Low, James Rea Jr.

Book B, page 14. Gift Deed of John Hays & wife Margatet to John

Lewis in consideration of love and affection 261 A adj William Mater, Widow Boyd, Pritchet, being part of grant to sd Hays in 1783. Sept. 6, 1787. John Hallum, John Dilworth, James Glass.

Book B, page 15. William Patterson to Nicholas McCubbin for 20 pds 238 A on Wolf Island Cr adj Mark London, William Stubblefield. 1787. Abner Parrott, Joseph Clark.

Book B, page 16. Joseph Manoca of Surry Co. to John Webster for 50 pds 150 A in Rockingham and Guilford on br of Belews Cr, part of tract granted by Nathaniel Gadberry. Sept. 15, 1787. James Reagan, Cornelius Cook.

Book B, page 17. Thomas Holgan of Orange Co. to Moses Yell for 50 pds 72 A on Gr Troublesome Cr adj Yell's own line, James McNealey. Dec. 21, 1787. A. Philips, William Jones, James Guby.

Book B, page 18. Peter Perkins to George Hairston and John Marr of Henry Co., Va. for 3,000 640 A on both sides Big Troublesome Cr, being grant to Archibald Lytle and then sold to sd Perkins. 1788. James McCleland, William Trammill.

Book B, page 19. William Baker to Philip Jenkins of Pittsylvania Co., Va. for 36 pds 180 A on Hogans Cr. July 14, 1787. Jno. Hunter, Robt. Williams, Jno Dabney.

Book B, page 20. Elizabeth Savage to Edward Taylor for 50 pds 150 A on Hogans Cr. May 15, 1787. Daniel Atkins, Thomas James.

Book B, page 21. John Linder & wife Mary to Laurance Bankson for 20 pds 100 A on S side Thrashers Fork Cr adj Bankson's own line. May 22, 1786. Charles Cantrell, Isaac Cantrell, John Mitchell.

Book B, page 22. Mary Elliot to Lawrence Bankson for 40 pds 121 A on Little Rockhouse Cr adj David Lovell, Charles Galloway. May 7, 1787. Edward Robison, Andrew Robison.

Book B, page 23. John Sims to William Norton for 100 pds 400 A on Wolf Island Cr adj Parrott. Feb. 10, 1788. Const. Perkins, Richard Allen, Philip Jenkins.

Book B, page 24. John Thrasher Sr. to John Thrasher Jr. for 200 pds 220 A on Lickfork of Hogans Cr adj Thomas Sparks, Joseph Cloud, upper part of grant by Granville to sd John Thrasher Sr. Feb. 17, 1788. Jas. C. Thrasher, Isaac Thrasher, William Bethell.

Book B, page 25. William Wallice to John Stanford for 130 pds 202 A on S side Gr Troublesome Cr adj John Hollock, Stanford's own land, Michael Caffey, James Johnson, being part of grant to John Wallice that descended to William Wallice as Heir at law at death of John Wallice. Jan. 31, 1788. A. Philips, Cynthia Philip.

Book B, page 26. Bridgar Hainey of Wilks Co., Ga. to Alexander McClaran for 50 pds 240 A on both sides Great Rockhouse Cr. adj James Sanders. Jan. 26, 1788. Tho. Henderson, John Glenn Jr., James Rogers.

Book B, page 27.   John Scroggin to Jacob Cantrell for 200 pds 300 A on Wolf Island Cr adj Reubin Dicson, Edward Williams, Robt & Charles Cantrell.   Apr. 20, 1787.   Wm. Moberley, Edward Williams, Tho. Pound.

Book B, page 28.. James Pratt (son of John Pratt dec'd) to Elizabeth Strong for 40 pds 50 A adj Turbefield Barns.   Feb. 23, 1788.   John Strong, Jas. Holderness.

Book B, page 29.   James Jackson to James Meloy for 30 pds 145 A on Hickry Cr of Mayo R adj Surry Co. line, Thomas Crawley, John Ruson.   Sept. 1, 1787.   Geo. Peay, Abner Johnson, John Peay.

Book B, page 30.   John Hancock of Randolph Co. to Ijah Hancock for 50 pds 104 A adj Moravian line, Samuel Smith, William Spire, William Taylor.   Mar. 20, 1787.   William Hubbard, Isham Hancock, John Carman.

Book B, page 32.   Samuel Watt to Jacob Been for 50 pds 147 A on Hogans Cr.   1787.   Edward Scott, William Loftis.

Book B, page 33.   Thomas Holgan of Orange Co. to William Jones for 20 pds 32 A adj Dominick Highland, Andrew Boyd.   Dec. 21, 1787.   A. Philips, Moses Yell, James McNealey.

Book B, page 34.   John May Esq., Sheriff, to Walter Martin for 150 pds paid to William Plumbley 200 A on Piney Cr seized from Samuel Lane by writ of Fieri Facias directed to Sheriff by Thomas Henderson, Clerk of Court.   Nov. 29, 1787.

Book B, page 36.   Henry Chambles to Samuel Morgin of Caswell Co. for 50 pds 148 A on Piney fork of Town Cr adj John Simmons, Robert Coleman.   Dec. 29, 1786.   John Hunter, Jr., Robt. Coleman.

Book B, page 37.   John Wall to James Wardlaw for 3 pds 3 A, being part of tract of 100 A granted to sd Wall on Gr Rockhouse Cr. Feb. 10, 1787.   Tho. Pound, Luke Bernard, John Hendrickson.

Book B, page 38.   George Peay to John May for 57 pds 143½ A on N side of Dan R adj May's line, Galloway's line, Peay's line. Jan. 19, 1788.   A. Philips, David Walker.

Book B, page 39.   Zachariah Standley of Louisa Co., Va. grants Power of Atty to William Johnson to make deed to Alexander McClaran for 130 A on upper Hogans Cr adj John Oliver, Robert Gilliland.   May 12, 1785.   Gideon Johnson, Peter Johnson, Isaac Whitworth.

Book B, page 40.   George Martin of Montgomery Co., Va. to Agnes Maccabroy for 45 pds 200 A on Haw River adj Edward Richardson. Sept. 30, 1787.   John McAbroy, Joseph Cowan, Wm. Coleman.

Book B, page 41.   John Reagon to Alexander Martin for 40 pds 40 A on E side Hogans Cr, Roberts old mill, James Martin, sd Reagon's own line.   Nov. 1786.   Tho. Henderson, Leonard Barker.

Book B, page 42.   William Wallice to John Hollock for 50 pds 100 A on S side Bigg Troublesome Cr adj William Matear, part of tract that descended to sd Wallice from John Wallice as Heir at law.   Feb. 18, 1788.   A. Philips, Mary Jones, Hanah Philips.

Book B, page 44. John May Esq., Sheriff to John Cummings for 33 pds 400 A on upper Hogans Cr adj Michael Thomas, being land seized by order of Court and sold to highest bidder to satisfy debt of Thomas Bowen to John Cummings, Executor of Hugh Blair dec'd. Aug. 28, 1787.

Book B, page 46. George Martin of Montgomery Co., Va. to Edward Richardson for 60 pds 200 A on Haw R. Sept. 30, 1787. John McAbroy, Wm. Robinson, Joseph Cowan.

Book B, page 47. Robert Nelson "hath granted and made over" to John and Moses Nelson 225 A at fork of Jacobs Cr. Nov. 12, 1787. John McNairy.

Book B, page 48. George Martin of Montgomery Co., Va. to Agnes McAbroy for 60 pds 350 A on Haw R. Sept. 30, 1787. John McAbroy, Wm. Robinson, Joseph Cowan.

Book B, page 49. Zachariah Bryant of Sullivan Co. to John London for 30 pds 165 A of 400 A granted to Briant in 1783 on both sides Stones fork of Wolf Island Cr. Nov. 3, 1787. John C. Thrasher, John Odell, Benjn. Parrott.

Book B, page 50. John Allen Senr. to John Allen Junr. for 50 pds 157 A on Little Troublesome Cr and Hogans Cr adj William Walker, Thomas Conner. Sept. 3, 1787. William Philips, John Herron.

Book B, page 51. James Warmock to Francis Fare for 70 pds 163 A on Belews Cr adj John Southerland, Drewry Hutchings. May 28, 1787.

Book B, page 52. Stephen Sephew to Severangan Bull for 150 pds 345 A on both sides Little Rockhouse Cr adj John Jones, William Proctor, John Abbet, being part of grant to Benjamin Silman. Nov. 24, 1787. A. Philips, John Abbit, John Harding.

Book B, page 53. Lucy Rainey to William Winstead of Pittsylvania Co., Va. for 120 pds Va. money 200 A on S side Buffalo Island Cr adj Henry Scales, John Strong, John Simmons, Michael Thomas. Oct. 10, 1787. Philemon Perkins, Reubin Curtis, Lois Rainey, James Colquitt, Joseph Brim, Rice Brim.

Book B, page 54. Miner Marsh to Alexander McClaron for 150 pds 50 A on Gr Rockhouse Cr adj William Jones, James Sanders. Oct. 30, 1787. A. Philips, William Johnson, William Fowler.

Book B, page 55. John Scroggin to Edward Williams for 100 pds 150 A on Wolf Island Creek adj James Cantrell. Apr. 18, 1787. James Williams, William Mobley.

Book B, page 57. John Allen Sr. to Thomas Conner for 50 pds 140 A on Hogans Cr adj Allen, Andrew Martin, John Allen Jr. Aug. 30, 1787. Joseph McCullough, John Herron.

Book B, page 58. Thomas Young to Andrew Fargis of Halifax Co., Va. for 130 pds 300 A on both sides Town Cr adj John Lovell. Jan. 2, 1784. Wm. Stephen, John Buckanon, Samuel Slydeln.

Book B, page 59. Charles Toney to Thomas Raffety for 5 pds 50 A
on Town Cr. Nov. 28, 1787.

Book B, page 60. Isaac Vernon to Richard, Elizabeth and Nancy
Vernon, orphans of Thomas Vernon dec'd for 20 pds 136 A on N
side Mayo River adj Nehemiah Vernon, John and Isaac Vernon (orphans of Joseph Vernon), Samuel Dalton. Aug. 15, 1787. Richard
Vernon, John Joyce, William Barnes.

Book B, page 61. Henry Burch to Reuben Jackson for 100 pds 100
A on S side Mayo R adj Joel Gibson. Nov. 20, 1786.

Book B, page 62. Thomas Pound to Charles Galloway and Constant
Perkins of Pittsylvania Co., Va. for 5 sh 50 A on Big Rockhouse
Cr adj Charles Mitchel. Aug. 28, 1787. B. C. Lacy, John Odell,
Rich. Marr.

Book B, page 63. William Hunt Allen of Buckingham Co., Va. to
Philip Jacob Irion of Bedford Co., Va. for 800 pds Va. money 300
A on N side Dan R adj Valentine Allen. Oct. 8, 1784. Tho. Hen-
derson, R. Martin.

Book B, page 64. Constant Perkins of Pittsylvania Co., Va. and
Charles Galloway to the Justices and their successors in office
for 5 sh 1 A for the use and benefit of the Publick on E side of
Big Rockhouse Cr and including the Courthouse, Prison and Stocks.
Aug. 28, 1787. A. Philips, Jno Wilson, Jno. Odineal.

Book B, page 66. John Brison of Surry Co. to Henry Burch for
100 pds 400 A on Mayo River below mouth of Buffalo Cr adj Joel
Gibson, Andrew Gibson. Mar. 7, 1786. Reuben Jackson, Andrew
Gibson, David Clark.

Book B, page 67. John Duncan to Peter Scales for 100 pds 150 A
on S side Mayo R adj Isham Sharp, Joshua Smith, Isham Rice. Mar.
7, 1787. Joseph Scales, Robert Philips, Jno. Scales.

Book B, page 68. George Joyce and wife Delilah to James Joyce
for 155 pds Va. money 240 A on Mayo R adj Deatherage, Nehemiah
Vernon. Mar. 19, 1787. Allen Dodd, John Fields, Robert Warren.

Book B, page 69. James Brison of Surry Co. to Henry Burch for
20 pds 52 A adj Brison, William Moor. Mar. 7, 1786. Andrew
Gibson, Reuben Jackson, David Clark.

Book B, page 71. Thomas McCullock to William Philips for 50 pds
162 A on Hogans Cr adj McCullock. Aug. 29, 1787. A. Philips,
Walter Martin.

Book B, page 72. Mary Fulkerson to Thomas Chambers for 100 pds
385 A on Lickfork of Hogans Cr adj William Chambers, Thomas
Mullins. Aug. 28, 1787. Samuel Bethell, William Mount.

Book B, page 73. Samuel Bethell to William Bethell for 40 pds
30 A on W side of Lickfork of Hogans Cr adj Flower Swift, Isaac
Dorriss, Thomas Mullins. Feb. 12, 1787. Jerre Sparks, John
Perks, Richard Stubblefield.

Book B, page 74. Thomas McCullock to Wm. McCullock for 50 pds

136 A on Hogans Cr adj John Philips, John Allen. Aug. 29, 1787.
A. Philips, William Philips.

Book B, page 75. Thomas McCullock to John Philips for 50 pds
100 A on Hogans Cr adj John Hodge, John Allen. Aug. 29, 1787.
A. Philips, William Philips.

Book B, page 76. James Jones & wife Pricilla to William Bethell
for 200 pds 200 A on Hogans Cr adj Bethell's own land. Mar. 7,
1786. Manlove Torrant, Samuel Bethell.

Book B, page 77. Andrew Martin & wife Ann to John Allen for 50
pds 125 A on Prewets fork of Hogans Cr adj George Roland, Thomas
Preston, John Hodge. Aug. 30, 1787. Walter Martin, John Martin.

Book B, page 78. John Thompson of Guilford Co. to Salathiel
Newmam for 120 pds 300 A on Little Troublesome Cr adj Adam Hol-
ker, Wm. Spirse. Nov. 11, 1787. Shiveral Garner, William Ferr
Thompson.

Book B, page 79. James Hunter to John Vaughn for 40 pds Va.
money 150 A on Bever Island Cr adj Wimbush, Hughs. May 20, 1787.

Book B, page 80. Mary Elliot to Andrew Robertson for 5 pds 150
A on both sides Little Rockhouse Cr adj William Elliot. Aug.
28, 1787. Tho. Pound, Nicholas Davis, William Odell.

Book B, page 81. John Jones to Matthew Peggs for 10 pds 100 A
on both sides Reed Cr adj sd Jones, William Walker. Nov. 22,
1786. David Watkins, Martha Covington.

Book B, page 83. Thomas Chambers to William Mount for 100 pds
100 A on Lickfork of Hogans Cr adj William Chambers dec'd, Publick road by sd Chambers Mill, Mary Fulkerson. Aug. 24, 1787.
Mary Fulkerson, Samuel Bethell.

Book B, page 84. Zachariah Stanley of Louisa Co., Va. to John
Oliver for 53 pds 100 A on S side Dan R and Little Hogans Cr.
May 23, 1786. Jno. Hunter Jr.

Book B, page 85. James Roberts to Naaman Roberts for 5 pds 134
A on both sides Clouds Cr of Dan R adj George Carter, James
Roberts. Feb. 3, 1786. Philip Rose, Ezra Roberts.

Book B, page 86. John May to Sneed Strong for 88 pds 50 A on
Dan R and Schoolhouse Cr adj sd Mays, John Simmons, Roberts.
May 20, 1787.

Book B, page 87. George Carter of Montgomery Co., Va. to James
Galloway for 250 pds 200 A on Clouds Cr on S side of Dan R adj
James Roberts, part of grant to sd Carter in 1780. May 13, 1786.
Turbefield Barnes, Richard Sharp, Robt. Galloway.

Book B, page 88. Jesse Broughton of Nash Co. to Peter Perkins
for 50 pds 500 A on Little Troublesome Cr adj Hugh Harkins,

Benjamin Granger, William Plumley. May 1, 1786. Nathaniel Lanier, Jacob Crockrell, Job Broughton.

Book B, page 89. John Morton to Peter Perkins for 1200 pds 300 A on S & SE sides Dan R adj John Walker, Watkins old line. Mar. 25, 1786. Nathaniel Scales, Jeremiah Norris, Geo. Peay.

Book B, page 91. Thomas Henderson to John Cunningham for 10 pds 38 A on N side Gr Troublesome Cr adj sd Henderson, James Grant, sd Cunningham. Nov. 30, 1786.

Book B, page 92. Jacob Caton to John Hampton for 30 pds Va. money 240 A on N Side Dan R and on Whetstone Cr adj John Lemons, John May. May 23,1786. Gideon Johnson Sr., Allen Walker, Mark Hardin Sr.

Book B, page 93. William Plumley & wife Phebe to Andrew Martin Sr. for 100 pds 223 A on both sides Piney Br adj sd Plumley, Lane, Soloman West. Apr. 1, 1786. Soloman Webster, Walter Martin.

Book B, page 94. Jeremiah Thacker to William Crockrell for 600 pds 150 A on Long Br of Lickfork of Hogans Cr adj William Chambers, Mary Fulkerson. May 26,1786. Jno. Odineal, Joseph McClain, William Bethell.

Book B, page 95. State of N.C. to John Simmons Sr. 300 A on Horse Patter Cr. Oct. 14, 1783.

Book B, page 96. State of N.C. to Andrew & David Scott 37 A on Little Troublesome Cr adj John Harris, Andrew Scott dec'd, Tyre Hairiss. Apr. 15, 1788.

Book B, page 97. State of N.C. to John Robertson 50 A on Haw R adj William Robertson, William Hall, Edward Taylor. July 11,1788.

Book B, page 98. State of N.C. to John Robertson 50 A on Haw R adj William Robertson, William Hall, Edward Taylor. July 11,1788.

Book B, page 99. State of N.C. to Matthew Mills 451 A on W side of Wolf Island Cr adj Ashon Bryant, John McCubbin, Benjamin Parrott, Richard Marr, Mill's own line. May 16, 1787.

Book B, page 100. State of N.C. to Thomas Pound 200 A on Big Rockhouse Cr adj Charles Mitchell, Luke Bernard. Apr. 15, 1788.

Book B, page 101. State of N.C. to Robert Barr 300 A on both sides Little Troublesome Cr adj Peter King, Hugh Harkins. Apr. 15, 1788.

Book B, page 102. State of N.C. to Mary Porter 300 A on Gr Troublesome Cr adj Francis McBride, Richard Henderson, John Young. Apr. 15, 1788.

Book B, page 103. State of N.C. to Thomas Connar 500 A on Little Troublesome Cr adj Harris, Walker. May 16, 1787.

Book B, page 104. State of N.C. to John Taylor 199 A on Mill Cr. of Haw R adj George Adams. May 16, 1787.

Book B, page 105. State of N.C. to George Adams 200 A on Mill

Cr adj John Taylor, Caswell County, George Hamilton. May 16, 1787.

Book B, page 106. State of N.C. to Isaac Cantrell 220 A on Wolf Island Cr adj John Linder, John Bankson. July 18, 1788.

Book B, page 107. State of N.C. to John Cummings 50 A on Jacobs Cr adj own land. July 11, 1788.

Book B, page 108. State of N.C. to John Wafford 62 A on Troublesome Cr adj Thomas Holgan, James Johnston, Michael Caffey. Apr. 15, 1788.

Book B, page 109. State of N.C. to John Cummings 100 A on Gr Troublesome Cr adj own land. July 11, 1788.

Book B, page 110. State of N.C. to John Stanford 48 A on Gr Troublesome Cr adj William Robinson, William Williams, Widow Turner, William Buckanon. July 11, 1788.

Book B, page 111. State of N.C. to Thomas King 200 A on Jacobs Cr adj Joseph Cunningham, James Brown. Apr. 15, 1788.

Book B, page 112. State of N.C. to John Hendrickson 350 A on both sides Little Rockhouse Cr adj David Caldwell, Bell, Kimbrell. May 16, 1787.

Book B, page 113. State of N.C. to Andrew Wilson 135 A on Haw R adj own land, Isaac Dilworth, Joseph Pain, William Williams. May 16, 1787.

Book B, page 114. State of N.C. to George Kimbal 640 A on Little Rockhouse Cr & Big Rockhouse Cr adj Joseph Burton. May 16, 1787.

Book B, page 115. State of N.C. to James Grant 250 A on Wolf Island Cr and Town Cr adj John Hendrickson, William Mobley, Harris. July 11, 1788.

Book B, page 116. State of N.C. to Andrew Scott 80 A on Little Troublesome Cr adj own land. May 16, 1787.

Book B, page 118. State of N.C. to Levy King 150 A on Troublesome Cr adj Thomas Massey, Alexander Brown. Apr. 15, 1788.

Book B, page 119. State of N.C. to Michael Caffey 50 A adj own land, Patrick Mullins. Apr. 15, 1788.

Book B, page 120. State of N.C. to John Thomas 100 A on Meadow Br of Jacobs Cr adj Isaac Perriman. July 11, 1788.

Book B, page 121. State of N.C. to William Hunt 408 A on both sides Saura Town Cr of Dan R and Town Cr adj Farlow. Nov. 8,1784.

Book B, page 122. State of N.C. to John Cummings 85 A S of Big Troublesome Cr adj own land, James Delay, Thomas Lomax. July 11, 1788.

Book B, page 123. State of N.C. to William Collins 200 A on Hogans Cr adj William Savage, John Herbin, Samuel Watt, Thomas Reading. May 16, 1787.

Book B, page 124. State of N.C. to Mary Patrick 189 A on Mill Cr of Haw R adj George Martin, Benjamin Dilworth, James Patrick. May 16, 1787.

Book B, page 125. State of N.C. to Robert Walker 259 A on Big Rockhouse Cr adj Thomas Pound, Mitchel's Cr and line. May 16, 1787.

Book B, page 126. State of N.C. to John Lain 400 A on Haw R adj Benjamin Dilworth, George Martin, Elisha Briggs. July 11, 1788.

Book B, page 127. State of N.C. to James Richey 50 A on Long Br of Dan R adj Adam Tate, John Silman. May 16, 1787.

Book B, page 128. State of N.C. to Luke Bernet 70 A on Gr Rockhouse Cr adj own land. May 16, 1787.

Book B, page 129. State of N.C. to John Wallas 400 A on S side Big Troublesome Cr adj William Roberson. May 16, 1787.

Book B, page 130. State of N.C. to Francis McBride 96 A on Troublesome Cr adj own land, James Flack. April 15, 1788.

Book B, page 131. State of N.C. to Samuel Martin 150 A on S side Jacobs Cr and on both sides Pounding Mill Br adj Isaac Rolston. July 11, 1788.

Book B, page 132. State of N.C. to John Daniel Garner 100 A on Troublesome Cr adj Thomas Lomax, David Peoples. July 11, 1788.

Book B, page 133. State of N.C. to Matthew Mills 400 A on brs of Wolf Island Cr adj own land, Hugh Challice, Wyatt Stubblefield. May 16, 1787.

Book B, page 134. State of N.C. to Samuel Shortt 300 A on Jacobs Cr adj own land, Charles Bruce. Nov. 8, 1784.

Book B, page 135. State of N.C. to William Mateer 613 A on both sides Troublesome Cr adj William Jones. Apr. 15, 1788.

Book B, page 136. State of N.C. to Patrick Hays 200 A on both sides Hogan Cr adj James Bates. May 16, 1787.

Book B, page 137. State of N.C. to John Hogge 640 A on headwaters of Hogan Cr adj Paynes Mill, McCollock, Allen, Wall. May 16, 1787.

Book B, page 138. State of N.C. to Michael Caffey 150 A on Jacobs Cr adj Peter Mitchell, Philip's Road. July 11, 1788.

Book B, page 139. State of N.C. to James Patrick 54 A on S side Haw R and own land, Burwell Peoples. Apr. 15, 1788.

Book B, page 140. State of N.C. to Martha Fletcher 200 A on Wolf Island adj Samuel Watt, John Odineal, William Bethell. May 16, 1787.

Book B, page 141. State of N.C. to Isham Browder 200 A on S side Wolf Island Cr adj John Smith. May 16, 1787.

Book B, page 142. State of N.C. to Isham Browder 168 A on N side Wolf Island Cr adj Edward Stubblefield, John Linder, Bankston. Nov. 8, 1784.

Book B, page 143. State of N.C. to Isham Browder 200 A on Wolf Island Cr adj William Garrott, John Cantrell. Nov. 8, 1784.

Book B, page 144. State of N.C. to John McPeck 150 A on Upper Hogans Cr adj Michael Thomas, Benjamin Bowen. Nov. 8, 1784.

Book B, page 146. State of N.C. to James Lanier 400 A on both sides Troublesome Cr adj Francis McBride, Richard Henderson, John Cunningham, John Falconer, Thomas Henderson. Apr. 15, 1788.

Book B, page 147. State of N.C. to William Hall 250 A on Country line Cr adj Thomas Hardin, William Walker, William Robertson, John Taylor, Caswell County line. July 11, 1788.

Book B, page 148. State of N.C. to John Purtell 190 A on Gr Rockhouse Cr adj own land, John McCarel, McCarlister, Thomas Larkin, Thomas King. May 16, 1787.

Book B, page 149. State of N.C. to John Pirkle 200 A on Gr Rockhouse Cr adj Charles Mitchel, Aron William, John McCarel, Robert Walker. July 11, 1788.

Book B, page 150. State of N.C. to John Pirkle 120 A on head-waters of Piney Cr adj own land, McCollister. May 16, 1787.

Book B, page 151. State of N.C. to Batte Cocke, Hopkins, Theophilus, John & William Lacy, Orphans of Theophilus Lacy dec'd 437 A on both sides Dan R adj own land, Francis Ford, Nicholas Larimore. May 29, 1788.

Book B, page 152. State of N.C. to Isaac Periman 200 A on Brushy fork of Jacobs Cr adj own land, John Shepherd. May 16, 1787.

Book B, page 153. Daniel Allen Jr. & mother Sarah Allen, Widow of John Allen dec'd to Joseph Clark for 100 pds in gold & silver 83 A on Hogans Cr adj Daniel Allen Sr., George Allen, William Clark Jr., sd Clark's own land. Aug. 5, 1788. Isaac Clark, John Pritchett, Michael Leathers.

Book B, page 154. John Matlock & wife Sarah to Joseph Clark for 20 pds 100 A on Hogans Cr adj Matlock's own land, Thacker. Nov. 25, 1789. Isaac Clark, William Clark Jr.

Book B, page 156. William Spiers of Surry Co. to John Harris for 160 pds 300 A on Lickfork of Hogans Cr adj John Hancock, William Overby, Silas Brock, Isham Browder. June 5, 1788. Daniel Atkins, Salathiel Newnam, Mary Newnam.

Book B, page 157. Joel Thomas to Charles Galloway & Company for 20 pds 150 A on E fork Sharps Cr of Dan R. Dec. 14, 1787. Jno. Campbell, James Scales, Milchejah Spragins.

Book B, page 159. Jesse Thomas, Joel Thomas & William Thomas to Charles Galloway & Co. for 100 pds Va. money 750 A on Whetstone Cr of Dan R adj Turbefield Barnes. Dec. 4, 1787. Jno. Campbell, James Scales, Melchijah Spragins.

Book B, page 161. Thomas Norris to Leavin Mitchel for 100 pds 227 A on both sides Town Cr adj Mitchel, Thomas Young, being part of grant Oct. 14, 1783 to James Norris. Oct. 16, 1787. A. Phillips, Joseph Williams.

Book B, page 163. John Conn to George Rowland for 30 pds 37½ A on Haw R adj sd Rowland. May 19,1788. George Rowland, James Nickell.

Book B, page 164. Charles Toney to Thomas Raffety for 75 pds 150 A on Town Cr adj Norris. Jan. 1, 1787. Richard Stubblefield Jr., Isham Simmons, Fanney Howerton.

Book B, page 165. Isham Simmons to Constant Perkins of Pittsylvania Co., Va. for 45 pds 300 A on Burchfields fork of Wolf Island Cr. May 1, 1788. Robert Galloway, Jno Challes, Isaac Clark.

Book B, page 166. Sarah Powell to Joshua Smith for 75 pds 106 A on Mayo Mt. adj sd Smith, Sarah Powell, near Mountain Meeting House. Jan. 22, 1787. Richard Bondurant, Francis Bondurant, Jesse Siers.

Book B, page 168. Joseph Williams to William Parks for 50 pds 120 A on N side Mayo River adj sd Williams, Joel Gibson. July 15, 1788. William Mobley, James Asberry.

Book B, page 170. Thomas Holgan of Orange Co. to James McNealy for 50 pds 127 A on Gr Troublesome Cr adj Moses Yell. Dec. 21, 1787. A. Philips, Jurat, Moses Yell, William Jones.

Book B, page 171. Jeremiah Poston of Caswell Co. to James Appleton for 25 pds 50 A on waters of Country line adj sd Poston and sd Appleton. Feb. 1789. John Williams.

Book B, page 172. Henry Hays & wife Nancy to Dennis Kelley for 100 pds 70 A adj sd Kelly, Moravin line, Joseph Griffin. Jan. 14, 1789. Joseph Griffin.

Book B, page 174. William Burton & wife Ann of Pittsylvania Co., Va. to John Walker for 50 pds 250 A on Wolf Island Cr adj Allen Williams, Luke Bernard, land granted May 16, 1787 to Joseph Burton. May 27, 1788. Robt. Galloway, Nathl. Linder, James Saunders.

Book B, page 175. Stephen Sephew to John Jones for 20 pds 23 A on both sides Little Rockhouse Cr. Feb. 21, 1789. A. Philips, Alem B. Williams.

Book B, page 177. Robert Barr to Andrew & David Scott for 100 pds 300 A on both sides Little Troublesome Cr adj Peter King, Hugh Harkins, John Haines, Robert Martin. Feb. 20, 1789.

Book B, page 178. Alexander McClaran to Mason French for 66 pds 6 sh 8 p 145 A on Brushey fork of Gr Rockhouse Cr adj William Jones, James Saunders. Oct. 9, 1788. A. Philips, William Clark, Jr.

Book B, page 179. Zachariah Bryan of Sullivan Co. to George Ward of Pittsylvania Co., Va. for 100 pds 100 A on Stoney Cr adj Matthew Mills, John Lunnon, Philip Larimore, Samuel Brown. Nov. 1, 1788. George Adams, Philip Laremore, John Perkins.

Book B, page 181. John Young & wife Comfort to Henry King for 30 pds 200 A on both sides Rockhouse Cr adj line of David Pursell dec'd, Robert Small, Abraham Philips. Jan. 19, 1789. A. Philips, David Scales, Jeremiah West.

Book B, page 182. Nathaniel Linder & wife Mary to Thomas Larkin for 50 pds 100 A on Gr Rockhouse Cr. Feb. 4, 1789. A. Philips, Thomas King, Abraham Hendrickson.

Book B, page 184. Jeremiah Sparks & wife Mary to William Bethell for 120 pds 200 A on Hogans Cr adj Joseph McClain, James Horsford, Thos Mullins, Samuel Bethell, William Bethell, part of grant of 452 A to Thomas Sparks. Nov. 10, 1787. Richard Stubblefield, Moses Vincent, Samuel Bethell.

Book B, page 185. Jeremiah Sparks & wife Mary of Franklin Co., Ga. to William Bethell for 100 pds Va. money 202 A on Hogans Cr adj sd Bethell, Thrasher, Flower Swift, Mullin, part of grant to Thomas Sparks. Dec. 12, 1788. Isham Hancock, Milley Sparkes.

Book B, page 186. Archibald Yarbrough to Nathaniel Williams for 500 pds 564 A on Wolf Island Cr adj Jo Cook, Wyatt Stubblefield, Thrasher. Jan. 22, 1787. John Challes, Jas Sommers, Isham Dalton.

Book B, page 188. Lewis Irion & wife Charlotte to Charles Galloway for 500 pds sterling 696 A adj Turbefield Barnes, being land granted to Nicholas Perkins Dec. 21, 1761 in Roan Co. Feb. 18, 1789. Geo. Peay Sr., Henry Scales, M. Hardin Jr.

Book B, page 189. Geo. Peay & Henry Scales, Esqrs appointed by Court to secure oath from Charlotte Irion, wife of Lewis Irion that she signed above deed on her own free will.

Book B, page 190. James Holderness & wife Frances to Charles Galloway for 200 pds sterling for 301 A on Linville Cr adj Turbyfield Barnes. Feb. 18, 1789. Geo. Peay Sr., Henry Scales, M. Hardin Jr.

Book B, page 192. George Peay & Henry Scales, Esqrs appointed by Court to secure oath from Frances Holdiness, wife of James Holderness that she signed above deed of her own free will.

Book B, page 193. George Peay & Henry Scales certify that Frances Holderness, wife of James Holderness and Charlotte Irion, wife of Lewis Irion, voluntarily and of their own free will relinquished all their right of Dower to aforesaid tracts of land.

Book B, page 194. Mathew Sims to Charles Galloway, Gent. for 100 pds sterling 300 A on Lickfork of Buffalo Island Cr adj John Hill, William Lanston Lewis. Feb. 18, 1789.

Book B, page 195. Court appoints Joshua Smith and James Hunter, Esqrs to secure oath from Mary Dearing wife of John Dearing that she signed deed to William Dearing of her own free will. Aug. 24, 1789.

Book B, page 196. James Hunter and Joshua Smith certify signature of Mary Dearing, wife of John Dearing, on deed to William Dearing. Nov. 23, 1789.

Book B, page 197. Geo. Peay and Henry Scales certify that Sarah Lewis, widow of William Langston Lewis, and Mary Sims, wife of Mathew Sims, relinquish their right of Dower to land sold to Charles Galloway on Lickfork of Buffalo Island Cr. Feb. 1789.

Book B, page 197. John Taylor of Montgomery Co. to William Robertson for 42 pds 100 A on W fork of Mill Cr adj Edm. Haggard. Mar. 4, 1789. Peter Oneal, Thomas Philips, Jurat.

Book B, page 199. Adam Baker & wife Mary of Rutherford Co. to Nathaniel Linder for 165 pds 400 A on both sides Jacobs Cr. May 19, 1789. John Earle, William Baker, Adam Baker Jr.

Book B, page 200. Nathaniel Williams to Daniel Allen for 50 pds 50 A on a br of Hogans Cr adj George Allen, Joshua Allen. Mar. 11, 1789. Stewart Diamond, Soleman Allen, Nathl. Williams Jr.

Book B, page 202. Thomas Henderson to Thomas & James Oakley for 100 pds 400 A on Paw Paw Cr adj William Williams, William Kellum Sr. Nov. 1, 1786. T. Searcy.

Book B, page 204. Peter Oneal to Reuben Cochran for 43.6.8 82 A on a br adj David Settle, part of grant to Soloman Loftis 1783 bought by Oneal. May 29, 1787. Saml. Watt Jr., William Cockrill, William Hubbert.

Book B, page 205. Reuben Southern of Surry Co. to Joshua Smith for 5 pds 100 A on S side Dan R opposite Neale's Bent, adj line formerly called Hunter's line now called Peay's. July 21, 1787. James Rhodes, William Barns, Lewis Hobby Johnston.

Book B, page 207. Sarah Smith Sr. (by some called Sarah Powel) to Sarah Smith Jr. for 50 pds 146 A on top Mayo Mt adj Joshua Smith, Barnes. Dec. 31, 1787. Joshua Smith, John Whitworth, Vallentine Allen Jr.

Book B, page 209. William Reed of Pittsylvania Co., Va. to John Jones for 10 pds land on both sides Brushey fork of Reed Cr adj sd Reed, Col. James Martin in the Surry Co. line, Mathew Peggs. Aug. 23, 1788. Benjamin Reed, William Reed, Joseph Reed.

Book B, page 211. John Leak to Philip Rose & Thomas Rose for 340 pds 450 A on Matrimony Cr adj Reece Price, John Menzie. May 14, 1789. Leaner Bolling (her mark), Robert Saunders, Geo Peay.

Book B, page 212. Elizabeth Strong to James Rhodes for 50 pds land on Double Crs of Fishing Cr adj Thomas Grogan. Aug. 30, 1787. J. Holderness, Nathaniel Moxley.

Book B, page 214. Samuel Watt Jr. & wife Jean to John Watt for 100 pds 246 A on Hogans Cr adj Jacob Bean, being a grant to Samuel Watt Jr. in 1782. June 24, 1788. James Watt, John Watkins.

Book B, page 216. State of N.C. to Joseph Allen 161 A on Hogans Cr adj Joseph Payn, Joshua Wright, Walker. Apr. 15, 1788.

Book B, page 217. Peter Oneal to William Hubbart for 43.6.8 70 A on Prewits fork of Hogans Cr adj David Vaughan, David Settle. May 29, 1787. Saml. Watt Jr., William Cockrill, Reuben Cochran.

Book B, page 218. William Hornbuckle to George Hornbuckle for 46 pds Va. money 100 A on Country Line Cr adj Poston, Hugh Gwyn. May 1789.

Book B, page 219. John Taylor of Montgomery Co. to Edmund Hoggard of Caswell Co. for 200 pds land on Mill Cr adj Harris, George Adams, William Williams, William Robertson. Mar. 4, 1789. William Hornbuckle, Peter Oneal, Thomas Philips.

Book B, page 220. William Mateer to John Waughford for 200 pds 182 A adj James Wright, Vandergraph, Peter Misellit, Walter Denny. Feb. 2, 1789. A. Philips, Robert Martin.

Book B, page 222. William Wilson & wife Jane to Joshua Wright for 50 pds 200 A on Haw R adj Joseph Payne, Andrew Wilson, Thomas Dilworth. Dec. 26, 1787. Joseph Payne Jr.

Book B, page 223. Joseph Payne & wife Martha to Joshua Wright for 50 pds 100 A on Giles Cr of Haw R. Dec. 26, 1787. Jno. Stewart, Joseph Payne Jr.

Book B, page 224. George Allen & wife Nancy to Daniel Allen for 95 pds 105 A adj each others property and Nathl Williams. Sept. 8, 1788. David Settle, Benjamin Spencer, Thos Allen.

Book B, page 226. John Grogan of Henry Co., Va. to Elijah Harrison for 100 pds 100 A on Little Buffalo Cr of Matrimony Cr adj Henry Grogan. Aug. 19, 1788. Henry Grogan, Frederich Caller, John Elexander.

Book B, page 227. William Odel to William Hopper for 50 pds 100 A on Little Buffalo of Matrimony Cr adj sd Odel, land purchased from Henry Grogan. Jan. 29, 1789. Jesse Harris, Joseph Hopper.

Book B, page 229. John Savage to Joseph Garner for 100 pds land on Hogans Cr being tract formerly sold by Robert Jones to William Savage. Apr. 5, 1788. David Settle, Jesse Bateman, John Matlock.

Book B, page 230. James Holderness to Turbyfield Barnes for 100 pds 5 A adj sd Holderness. Nov. 3, 1787. Tho Henderson, Joshua Smith, M. Hardin Jr.

Book B, page 232. Asa Brasher to Turbyfield Barns for 110 pds land adj William Williams, Dan River Road, John Adkinson. July 8, 1787. Tho. Henderson, James Hunter.

Book B, page 235. Hugh Harkins & wife Sarah to Soloman Webster for 211 pds 422 A on Little Troublesome Cr adj Andrew Scott, Jesse Braughton, Mathew George, being land on which sd Harkins and wife Sarah formerly lived. Nov. 25, 1788.

Book B, page 236. Jeremiah Norris to John Simmons for 40 pds 100 A on both sides Piney fork of Town Cr adj David Lovel, Sarah Potter, Sam Simmons, John Simmons Jr., John Lovel.

Book B, page 237. Thomas Redin to William Washington for 65 pds 80 A adj William Savage, Samuel Watt. Mar. 1, 1787. Chas. Collings, Sherwood Nance.

Book B, page 238. Minos Cannon & wife Lettice of Guilford Co. to James Reed for 50 pds 197 A on Troublesome Cr, Cannons Spring Br, Kings Road adj Isaac Wright. Jan. 16, 1788. Jas. Mulloy, John Work.

Book B, page 240. Benjamin Gates to Turbyfield Barns for 100 pds Va. money 341 A on E side Mayo R on S side Mayo Mountain on road leading from Mountain Meeting House into road leading from Moravian Town to Petersburgh, adj Robert Axton, Richard Vernon, Robert Warren, Thomas Pratt, Sarah Powel (Sarah Smith). Nov. 20, 1787. Joshua Smith, Thomas Pratt, Joanna Vernon.

Book B, page 242. John Triplet of Caswell Co. and Thomas Redin to William Washington for 85 pds 100 A on both sides Hogans Cr adj Samuel Watt, the sd land formerly belonging to William Savage, later purchased by Zebulin Savage. Mar. 1, 1787. Thomas Key, Sherwood Nance, Wm. Ferguson Thompson.

Book B, page 243. Daniel Sillivant to Edward Daniel for 50 pds 100 A on Va. line & Stewarts Cr adj Farlour. Oct. 13, 1787. Frederich Caller, Henry Scales.

Book B, page 245. State of N.C. to John Lewis 150 A on Hogans Cr adj James Nichol, James McCaleb, Isaac Lowe, Joseph Payn. July 11, 1788.

Book B, page 246. John McCarroll of Surry Co. to John Granger for 80 pds 320 A on Wolf Island Cr adj Wardlow's Claim, Barnard's Claim, Harrison. Mar. 7, 1789. William Dobson, J.P., Benjamin Williams.

Book B, page 247. John McCarroll, Atty for Jarret Brannon to John Granger for 30 pds 100 A on Wolf Island Cr adj Luke Borner, William Young, John Bell, Brandon. Nov. 25, 1789.

Book B, page 248. Jarratt Brandon of Washington Co. grants Power of Atty to Jno. McCarrill Jr. of Guilford to sign over 100 A on Wolf Island Cr to Jno Granshaw. May 10, 1783. Isham Browder, Charles Harris.

Book B, page 249. Tyre Harris, Cornelus Dabney & Simpson Harris of Caswell Co. Exrs of Tyre Harris dec'd, to Martin Wisenor for 420 pds 612 A on N fork of Haw R adj Joseph Pinson. Jan. 3, 1788. R. Simpson, Robt. Harris, David Burton.

Book B, page 250. William Hall of Montgomery Co. to William Williams of Guilford Co. for 150 pds 150 A on head of Country Line Cr adj Thos. Harden, Haggard. Aug. 28, 1789. William Hornbuckle, Henry Harden, Hugh Gwyn.

Book B, page 251. Nathaniel Linder & wife Mary to Robert Pamplin for 100 pds 150 A on Big Rockhouse Cr adj Thomas King. Apr. 18, 1789. Tho. Pound, John Mount, Abner Lovel.

Book B, page 253. Isaac Periman to John Dever for 100 pds 200 A on Brushy fork of Jacobs Cr adj sd Periman, John Shepherd. July 25, 1788. John Shepherd, John Periman.

BOOK C

Book C, page 1. State of N.C. to Thomas Owens 100 A on Lickfork of Hogans Cr adj William Spears. June 27, 1793.

Book C, page 1. State of N.C. to Robert Nelson 140 A on E fork of Jacobs Cr adj Francis Young. March 21, 1789.

Book C, page 2. State of N.C. to William Miller 100 A on Piney Cr adj sd Miller, Robert Small. July 11, 1787.

Book C, page 3. State of N.C. to John Linder 100 A on Wolf Island Cr adj sd Linder, Widdow Browder. May 16, 1787.

Book C, page 4. State of N.C. to John Linder 400 A on Gumping Br of Wolf Island Cr adj line of Isham Browder dec'd. July 11, 1788.

Book C, page 5. State of N.C. to John Bankson 300 A on both sides Wolf Island Cr adj Browder, Charles Harris, Nathaniel New-nam. May 16, 1787.

Book C, page 6. State of N.C. to William Jones 150 A on Brushy fork of Rockhouse Cr adj Aron Allen, Adam Baker. July 11, 1788.

Book C, page 7. William Buckanon to John Hollock for 66 pds 13 sh 4 p 100 A on S side Troublesome Cr being part of tract grant-ed to John Wallace dec'd that descended to John Hollock, Heir at law of William Wallace. Nov. 16, 1789. Burrel Pegely, John Stanford.

Book C, page 9. Joseph Pain Johnson to William Hopper for 35 pds Va. money 150 A on Lumber Tree Br of Buffaloe Island on little Buffaloe of Matrimony Cr near Center Meeting House adj Joseph Hopper, Edward Daniel. Jan. 17, 1789. Allen Dodd, Joseph Hopper.

Book C, page 10. Isaac Wright of Guilford Co. to Robert Small for 180 pds 640 A on Gr Rockhouse Cr adj Abraham Phillips, John Young. Aug. 26, 1789. A. Philips, Tho. Pound, Joseph Clark.

Book C, page 11. William Walker to Sarah Stephen for 20 pds 100 A on Cyrbys Cr of Dan R adj sd Walker. Feb. 25, 1790. James Walker.

Book C, page 12. William Walker & wife Susana to Turbyfield Barns for sum 327 A on N side of Dan R adj line of Nathaniel Hoggates dec'd, Surry Co. 1790. T. Searcy.

Book C, page 13. Aaron Going to Turbyfield Barns for 200 pds 410 A on head of Matrimony Cr & head of Popaye Cr adj. Hamilton. Nov. 8, 1788. Gideon Johnson, Luci Thomas, Hardy Piner (?).

Book C, page 14. Richard Sharp & wife Elizabeth to Turbyfield Barns for 8 pds 11 A adj sd Barns. 1787. T. Searcy.

Book C, page 15. State of N.C. to John Harris 20 A on Wolf Is-land Cr adj John Cantrill, Thomas Owen. Nov. 27, 17__.

Book C, page 16. State of N.C. to Laurence Porter 640 A on Quaiquab Cr of Wolf Island Cr. July 11, 1788.

Book C, page 17. Isaac Wright of Guilford Co. to John Howell for 300 pds 322 A on both sides Troublesome Cr adj Moses Camp-bell, Benjamin Stone, William Thorp, Guilford Co. line. May 11, 1789. Minos Cannon, Asa Brasher.

Book C, page 18. Mason French to Mary Stratton for 66 pds 6 sh
8 p 145 A on both sides Brushey fork of Gr Rockhouse Cr adj
William Jones, Abraham Philips, James Sanders, being part of grant to Minor March. Feb. 25, 1790. A. Philips, Caleb Blagg, Alexr.
McClaren.

Book C, page 19. Henry Lanier of Davidson to Mary Dobins for 100
pds 170 A on Gr Troublesome Cr adj Richard Henderson, John Cunningham, Francis McBride. A. Philips Atty for Henry Lanier.
Feb. 1790. Tho. Henderson, Henry Brewer.

Book C, page 20. Zackariah Bryan of Green Co. to Phillamon Lar-
aimore for 40 pds 79 A on Stones Fork of Wolf Island Cr adj Edward Perkins, John Odineal, Joseph Cloud. Nov. 5, 1787. John
Odell, Saml. Brown, Richd. Larimore.

Book C, page 21. State of N.C. to William Cockrill 90 A on Long
Br of Lickfork adj sd Cockrill, Nathan Thacker. July 11, 1788.

Book C, page 22. State of N.C. to Archable Yarbrough 220 A on
Lickfork of Hogans Cr adj Stubblefield's old line. May 16,1787.

Book C, page 23. State of N.C. to Samuel Watts 200 A on Hogans
Cr adj sd Watt, Thomas Reding, Abraham Philips. July 11, 1788.

Book C, page 24. State of N.C. to Samuel Watt 100 A on E side
of Hogans Cr adj William Collins, Caswell Co. line. July 11,1788.

Book C, page 25. State of N.C. to Joshua Pruitt 32 A on Lickfork
adj John Smith, Moravian line. July 11, 1788.

Book C, page 26. State of N.C. to William Robertson 60 A on
head of Country Line Cr adj sd Robertson. July 11, 1788.

Book C, page 27. State of N.C. to Dominick Highland 88 A betw
the two Troublesome Crs adj Robert Corry, William Jones, Robert
Boak, Thomas Holgan, Andrew Boyd. July 11, 1788.

Book C, page 28. State of N.C. to Zebulon Savage 194 A on Pruitts
fork of Hogans Cr adj Widdow Savage, James Martin, John Thompson,
-Aaron Arnold. Nov. 8, 1784.

Book C, page 29. John Simmons of Burk Co. to James Nickell for
100 pds 200 A on Horsepasture Cr of Dan R & crossing one fork of
Town Cr adj Robert Cole. Sept. 29, 1789. John Simmons, John
Norris.

Book C, page 30. Philip Rose & Thomas Rose to John Leak for 340
pds 450 A on Matrimony Cr adj Reece Price, John Minzie. May 14,
-1789. Leaner Bolling, Robert Sanders, Geo. Peay.

Book C, page 31. State of N.C. to James Powell 240 A on Reedy
fork of Hogans Cr adj William Moss, Caswell Co. line, Wyat Stubblefield. July 11, 1788.

Book C, page 32. John Maxwell of Guilford Co. to James Smith
for 10 pds 29 A adj sd Smith, Pritchett, being part of grant to
Maxwell 1784. Aug. 3, 1789.

Book C, page 33. Thomas Dick of Guilford Co. to James Smith for 8 pds 131 A adj sd Smith, William Mateer, John McCibbon, Rev. James Campbell. May 25, 1789. Benjamin Spencer, William Walker.

Book C, page 34. John Williams, William Moore, Absolum Tatum to John Johnson for 100 pds 300 A on Haw R. Aug. 27, 1789.

Book C, page 35. Nathaniel Linder to Robert Galloway for 150 pds 200 A on Gr Rockhouse Cr adj George Kimble, Thomas Lerkin. Aug. 25, 1789. Lewis Peoples, Sampson Lanier.

Book C, page 36. Zebulon Savage to John Savage for 30 pds 100 A on Hogans Cr, a tract formerly granted to Robert Jones and sold to William Savage. May 14, 1786. "I Elizabeth Savage, widdow of William Savage Sr. hath sold....my thirds share of above tract." Samuel Watt Jr., Thomas Savage, Robert Duncum, John Hamilton, Robt. Craig.

Book C, page 37. Hance McKeen of Guilford Co. to George Harston of Henry Co., Va. for 25 pds 155 A on Paw Paw Cr of Mayo R adj Va. line, James Goings. Feb. 21, 1789. Patrick Nealy. W. Hamilton.

Book C, page 38. Benjamin Parrott to Abner Parrott for 200 pds 500 A on both sides Wolf Island Cr adj William Hill, Farlow, Jesse Hammon's Claim. May 9, 1789. Fields Nickols, Benjamin Parrott Jr.

Book C, page 39. Benjamin Parrott Sr. to Abner Parrott for 200 pds 200 A on both sides Wolf Island Cr adj Joshua Fenlie. May 29, 1789. Fields Nickols, Benjamin Parrott Jr.

Book C, page 40. Peter Oneal to Thomas Harding for 60 pds 60 A on Country Line Cr adj Jeremiah Poston, William Walker. 1790. Henry Harden, John Cox.

Book C, page 41. Thomson Harris to Theodrick Stubblefield for 50 pds 45 A on Pruets fork of Hogans Cr adj sd Harris. Oct. 3, 1787. Richard Stubblefield, William Bethell.

Book C, page 42. James Bruce of Green Co. to William Harrison for 30 pds 200 A on both sides Wolf Island Cr adj William Tranum, being tract granted Oct. 4, 1783 to Thomas Bruce. June 2, 1788. John Hunter Jr., Jo Terrill, John Simons.

Book C, page 43. John Simmons Sr. to John Simmons Jr. for 100 pds 300 A on Piney Fork. Oct. 31, 1788. Robt. Coleman, Jeremiah Norris, John Lovel.

Book C, page 44. William Mark Jr. to Joseph Clark for 50 pds 130 A on Hogans Cr adj sd Clark, Daniel Allen, Sammuel Watt, John Matlock, Nathaniel Williams. Feb. 22, 1790. Isaac Clark.

Book C, page 45. Robert Harris & wife Lucey to Samuel Watt Jr. for 120 pds 120 A on Pruets fork of Hogans Cr adj Abraham Philips, being land willed to sd Harris by his father Thompson Harris. Nov. 28, 1787. John Watt, Theodrick Stubblefield.

Book C, page 46. John Tomlinson to John Lain both planters of Guilford Co. for 50 pds 100 A on Lickfork adj Thomas Williams,

Hickman, Widdow Mullin, Burton, being tract granted to Thadeus Owen, thence to James Tomlinson, thence to John Tomlinson. Dec. 25, 1788. James Wright, James Tomlinson.

Book C, page 47. Dominick Highland to William Jones for 52 pds 88 A between two Troublesome Crs adj sd Jones, Robert Curry, Thomas Holgan. Feb. 19, 1790. A. Philips, Cynthia Philips, Peter Nance.

Book C, page 48. Job Loftis to William Hickman for 76 pds 90 A on Lickfork of Hogans Cr adj Moravian line. Feb. 18, 1789. John Hickman, Isiah Hancock, Thadeus Owen.

Book C, page 49. John Mount to James Bateman for 60 pds 100 A on Lickfork of Hogans Cr adj Henry Dixon, Jno Hancock. Oct. 31, 1789. Richard Thrasher, George Foot, Richard Stubblefield.

Book C, page 50. Thomas Caffey to John Caffey for 150 pds 253 A on S side Haw R adj sd John Coffey. Jan. 26, 1789. A. Philips, Michael Caffey.

Book C, page 51. State of N.C. to John Gibson 47 A on Buffalow Island Cr adj Winkfield Shropshire. Nov. 8, 1784.

Book C, page 52. State of N.C. to John Gibson 100 A on Buffalow Island Cr adj Winkfield Shropshire. Nov. 8, 1784.

Book C, page 53. State of N.C. to Hugh Kirk Patrick 240 A on Hogans Cr. July 11, 1788.

Book C, page 54. State of N.C. to Col. James Martin 200 A on Cokers Cr of Dan R adj Benjamin Gates, John Nelson, John Nelson Jr. May 16, 1787.

Book C, page 55. State of N.C. to James Martin 400 A on Hogans Cr of Dan R adj sd Martin, James Roberts. Nov. 27, 1789.

Book C, page 56. State of N.C. to James Martin 300 A on Bever Island Cr adj William Crump, John Scales, Samuel Hunter's Claim. Oct. 14, 1783.

Book C, page 57. State of N.C. to James Martin 400 A on Hogans Cr adj sd Martin. May 16, 1787.

Book C, page 58. Samuel Watt Senr to James Watt for 50 pds 246 A on Hogans Cr adj Jacob Been. Aug. 20, 1789.

Book C, page 59. Gift Deed of Joseph Pritchet Sr. to John Pritchett for natural love & affection 52 A on E side Haw R adj George Dilworth, William Wilson. Dec. 21, 1788. John Hallum, Rich. Borton.

Book C, page 60. Joseph Payne & wife Martha to William Clark for 100 pds 70 A on Hogan's Cr adj sd Payne. Mar. 13, 1790. Thomas Clark, Geo. Payne, Joseph Clark.

Book C, page 61. Peter Oneal & wife Elizabeth to Michael Leather for 40 pds 100 A on Hogans Cr. Nov. 30, 1789. Jere. Poston, James Walker.

Book C, page 62. John Odineal & wife Sarah to Joseph Newcomb for 100 pds 100 A on Quacquah Cr adj Samuel Watt, Thrasher, John London. Apr. 23, 1789. Robert W. Somerhays, Mary Mills, Christopher Dudley.

Book C, page 63. Zackariah Thacker & wife Susanah to John Horsford for 160 pds 200 A on Pruets fork of Hogans Cr adj Hanah Harris, Nathan Thacker, Road leading to Dixies Ferry, William Obannion. Sept. 1788. John Humphreys, Jno. Dill, Jno. Allison.

Book C, page 64. Elmore Walker to Shadrack Lewis for 30 pds 103 A on Jacobs Cr. Feb. 25, 1790. A. Philips, Stephen Mitchell, Caleb Blagg.

Book C, page 65. Martin Wisinor to William Walker for 140 pds 200 A on N side North fork of How R adj Joseph Pinson. April 30, 1790. Benjamin Spencer, James Walker.

Book C, page 66. William Young to Sutton McCollister for 35 pds 55 A adj sd Young. May 1, 1790. A. Philips, Nancy Loard.

Book C, page 67. Aneil (Arreil?) Fields to Benjamin Smith for 10 pds land on Pappaw Cr & Fishing Cr adj Drury Smith. Oct. 25, 1788. Joshua Smith, James Rhodes, John Gibson.

Book C, page 70. Philip Anglin of Henry Co., Va. to Benjamin Smith for 20 pds 40 A on both sides Fall Cr, Mayo R, Virginia line. Oct. 23, 1788. Francis Grogan, Joshua Malry, William Kellam, Daniel Goldsbay.

Book C, page 71. William Plumley of Burk Co. formerly of Rockingham Co., to Walter Martin for certain sum 200 A on N side Piney Cr adj John Mabery, Perkins. July 20, 1790. Denten Plumlee, John Boak.

Book C, page 72. William Bethell to William Daveie for 50 pds 100 A on Lickfork and Wolf Island Cr adj sd Bethell, Larken Peirpoint. Sept. 24, 1789. William McCollum, Martha McCollum.

Book C, page 73. William Chapman Sr. to William Chapman Jr. for 20 pds Va. money 100 A on Lickfork of Hogans Cr adj Thadeus Owen, John Smith, John Hancock. May 4, 1790. Thomas Sparks, Jesse Bateman, Thomas Chapman.

Book C, page 74. Isaac Philips of Tenese Co. to Mary Patrick for 56 pds 200 A on Gr Rockhouse Cr adj John Mounts, being tract granted 1784 to sd Philips. Aug. 24, 1790. Dan Atkins, John McCollester.

Book C, page 75. John McCarrell to lawful heirs and orphans of David Morris dec'd for 19 pds 50 A on Wolf Island Cr adj sd McCarrell, Jesse Harrison, James McCarrill. July 17, 1790. A. Philips, Tho. Pound, John Mount.

Book C, page 76. State of N.C. to John Joice 200 A on Jacobs Cr adj Caleb Blagg. July 11, 1788.

Book C, page 77. Lord Granville to Joseph Payne of Orange Co. for 10 sh sterling 160 A on S Fork of Hogans Cr. Dec. 6, 1761.

Book C, page 80. William Washington to James Dyar of Orange Co. for 1,000 pds 330 A on both sides Hogans Cr adj Samuel Watt, William Savage, Thomas Redin. Nov. 11, 1788. Elisha Dyar, John Carrington.

Book C, page 81. State of N.C. to William Johnston 250 A on N side Dan R adj sd Johnston, William Covinton, George Peay. ____ ___, 17__.

Book C, page 84. William Boyd & wife Rebecca to Stewart Diamond for 500 pds 229 A on Little Troublesome Cr. Feb. 8, 1791. William Bradberry, John Hallum, Samuel Watt.

Book C, page 85. Syrus Lightfoot Roberts to William Thornton Morton for 100 pds 300 A on E side Dan R adj Hunter, Hunters Mill Road, John Walker. March 3, 1790.

Book C, page 86. State of N.C. to Robert Cummings 150 A on Haw R adj sd Cummings, Malachi Reaves, David Love. May 16, 1787.

Book C, page 87. State of N.C. to Robert Cummings 100 A on Gr Troublesome Cr adj Samuel Lanier, John Bankson, Francis McBride. July 11, 1788.

Book C, page 88. State of N.C. to John Walker 190 A on Gr Rock-house Cr adj James Roberts, Thomas Carter. May 16, 1787.

Book C, page 89. State of N.C. to William Hitchcock a Private in Continental Line who has given & granted unto James Hunter Assignee 640 A in Davidson Co. on Spencer Cr adj George Purtle, Charles Dungith. Nov. 7, 1789.

Book C, page 90. State of N.C. to Abraham Philips 60 A on Wolf Island Cr adj James Wardlow, John McCarrell, William Harrison. May 16, 1787.

Book C, page 91. State of N.C. to Abraham Philips 100 A on Ho-gans Cr adj Thompson Harris. July 11, 1788.

Book C, page 92. State of N.C. to Abraham Philips 50 A on Gr Rockhouse Cr adj Samuel Henderson, Alexander Calbreath, Richard Mason. July 11, 1788.

Book C, page 93. State of N.C. to Abraham Philips 100 A on Gr Troublesome Cr adj Francis McBride, Isaiah McBride, James Mc-Cleland. July 11, 1788.

Book C, page 94. State of N.C. to Abraham Philips 200 A on Little Troublesom Cr adj John Hainey, Silathem Nunon (Newnam?), William Spiar, William Gorden. Nov. 27, 1789.

Book C, page 95. Notley Jordan to William Bethell for 40 pds 50 A on Wolf Island Cr adj Richard Marr. Feb. 25, 1791. John Matlock.

Flower Swift & wife Priscilla to William Bethell for 60 pds 54 A on Lickfork of Hogans Cr adj Peter Lewis, part of grant to John Mullin. Mar. 12, 1789. Job Loftis, Samuel Garrison, Vinea Swift.

Book C, page 97. Thomas Dilworth & wife Nancy to James Thompson for certain sum 200 A on br of lower Hogans Cr adj John Dilworth,

James Walker, being tract granted 1784 to Jean Dilworth. Feb. 28, 1791. George Dilworth, Lemuel Thompson.

Book C, page 98. John Pirkle to Thomas King Sr. for 10 pds 60 A on Gr Rockhouse Cr adj Thomas Larkin, Allen Williams, Sutton McColister. Mar. 8, 1791. A. Philips, Nathaniel Harrison, George Pirkle.

Book C, page 99. Joseph Payne to James Higgins for 50 pds 130 A on Haw R adj Abraham Philips, Joshua Wright, William Robertson. Feb. 26, 1791. Isaac Clark, Wm. Clark Sr.

Book C, page 100. Abraham Philips to Shiveral Garner for 40 pds 60 A on Little Troublesome Cr adj Silathem Nunon, William Spier, crossing road from Dixies Ferry to Ironworks. Aug. 10, 1790. Geo. Payne, Robert Martin.

Book C, page 101. Joshua Mayberry to Charles Galloway & Co. for 250 pds 732 A on N side Dan R on brs of Fowl & Pawpaw Cr adj William Kellam, William Hays, Drury Smith. Sept. 16, 1790. Joshua Smith, Charles Smith, Elizabeth Smith.

Book C, page 102. William Lemond & wife Elizabeth to Charles Moore for 120 pds 200 A on both sides Conners Br of Troublesome Cr adj Robert Barr, Mathew George, Mathew Amberson, Hugh Harkins. Apr. 4, 1790. John Lemond, James Flack.

Book C, page 103. James Craton of Mecklenburg Co. to Samuel Moore for 100 pds 200 A on S side Haw R, being part of grant to William Robertson. Feb. 11, 1790. Michael Caffey, Moses Yell, Geo. Roland.

Book C, page 104. Uriah Odell to Maynard Colley for 40 pds 100 A on br of Buffalo Island Cr adj Henry Scales. Feb. 11, 1791. Henry Grogan, Ezekel Calahan, Moses Land.

Book C, page 105. John Odineal to John Wilson of Pitsylvania Co., Va. for 100 pds 540 A on both sides Quackquay Cr of Wolf Island Cr adj Newcomb, London. Feb. 15, 1790. Geo Adams, Wm. Moore, T. Wislon Jr., Jno. Wilson Jr.

Book C, page 106. James Kelley to William Silman for certain sum 100 A on Long Br of Rockhouse Cr adj Abraham Philips. 1790. David Walker, Wm. Walker.

Book C, page 107. Namon Roberts & Ezra Roberts to Syrus Light-foot Roberts for 500 pds 640 A on E side Dan R adj James Roberts, Hunter, part of grant to James Roberts 1783. Oct. 1, 1790. Wm. Thornton Morton, Daniel Thompson, Elizabeth Roberts.

Book C, page 108. State of N.C. to Walter Hill 257 A on Haw R adj Campbell, Scott, John Caffey, John Stanford. July 11, 1788.

Book C, page 109. State of N.C. to Robert Payne 240 A on Wolf Island Cr adj Caswell Co. line. May 16, 1787.

Book C, page 110. State of N.C. to Joshua Wright 50 A on Hogans Cr adj sd Wright, Alexander Walker, John Hodges, Brumfield Ridley Esq. July 11, 1788.

Book C, page 111. State of N.C. to William Hubbard 360 A on Burchfields fork of Wolf Island Cr adj sd Hubbard, Abraham Spencer, Smith. May 16, 1787.

Book C, page 112. State of N.C. to William Hubbard 640 A on head of London Mill Cr & Stone fork of Little Town Cr. May 16, 1787.

Book C, page 113. State of N.C. to John Correy Sr. 7 A on S side Haw R adj sd Correy, John Wafford, Peter Mesellit. July 11, 1788.

Book C, page 114. State of N.C. to William Diamond 100 A on Vaughans Cr & Lickfork adj James Hays, David Settle, Moses Garrison. Nov. 24, 1790.

Book C, page 115. Isham Lanier & wife Caterine to Thompson Lanier for 100 pds 300 A on Hogans Cr adj William Cummings, John Atkinson, William Fleming, being grant 1782 to Asa Brasher. Oct. 23, 1790. Nathaniel Lanier, James Dobbins, Joseph Periman.

Book C, page 116. Robert Crump & wife Mary of Stokes Co. to William Asher for 10 pds 50 A on Long Br of Bever Island Cr adj Anthony Dearing, Stokes Co. line, Thomas Lovell. Aug. 16, 1790. John Vawter, John Robinson, William Crump.

Book C, page 117. James Brown Sr. to James Brown Jr. for 50 pds 100 A on Gr Troublesome Cr adj sd Brown, Richard Henderson, John Cunningham. Aug. 27, 1790. A. Philips, Cynthia Philips.

Book C, page 118. Charles Moore & William Blake to James Colley for 50 pds Va. money 150 A on Hickory Cr. May 20, 1791. Edm. Burton, James Hunter.

Book C, page 119. James Kelley to John Brown for 100 pds 100 A on Gr Rockhouse Cr adj Abraham Philips. May 23, 1791. William Bethell.

Book C, page 120. Luke Bernard to James Williams for 27 pds 10 sh 55 A on Wolf Island Cr being part of tract on which Elisha Bernard now lives adj Thomas Pound. Dec. 10, 1790. Benjamin Williams, Jacob Bernard.

Book C, page 121. Robinson Shackelford to Humphry Garrett of King & Queen Co., Va. for 3 pds 6 sh 8 p 100 A whereon stands a mill called Parrotts Upper Mill adj Richard Marr, Jo Griffin. Nov. 5, 1791. William Bethell. Moses Allen, Stephen Odear.

Book C, page 122. Robert Pamplin & wife Mary to George Pirkle for 100 pds 150 A on Big Rockhouse Cr adj Thomas King. Feb. 24, 1791. Joseph Linder, Mathias Mount.

Book C, page 123. John Grogan of Henry Co., Va. to Jesse Hinton for 100 pds 100 A on Little Buffelow Cr of Matrimony Cr adj Elijah Harrison. Aug. 24, 1790. Henry Grogan, William Grogan, Alee Grogan.

Book C, page 124. Samuel Young of Ab ille Co., S.C. to Thomas Blair for 50 pds land on S side Troublesome Cr. Dec. 27, 1790. James Hays, Wm. Graham, Thomas Blair.

Book C, page 125. David Peeples of Wilks Co., Ga. to Robert Small for 50 pds 300 A on Jacobs Cr adj Peoples, Samuel Love. Nov. 14, 1791. Nathan Massey, Henry Lanier, Hubbart Peeples.

Book C, page 126. David Peeples of Ga. to Robert Small for 100 pds 80 A on Jacobs Cr adj Thomas Allen. Nov. 4, 1791. Nathan Massey, Henry Lanier, Hubbard Peeples.

Book C, page 127. State of N.C. to William Hubbart 40 A on Lickfork of Hogans Cr adj Moses Garrison, Moravian line. Nov.17,1790.

Book C, page 128. State of N.C. to William Hubbert 47 A on Pruets fork of Hogans Cr adj sd Hubbard, David Settle. Nov. 17, 1790.

Book c, page 129. State of N.C. to George Hairston and John Marr, Assignees for Peter Perkins 100 A on Gr Troublesome Cr adj John Blackburn, Abraham Philips, line of James Lanier dec'd, John Black. Nov. 17, 1790.

Book C, page 130. State of N.C. to Robert Rollstone 200 A on Jacobs Cr adj Isaac Rollstone, Alexander Martin Esq. Apr.15,1788.

Book C, page 131. State of N.C. to Thomas Keys 98 A on Hogans Cr adj Joseph Garner, Caswell Co. line. Dec. 15, 1791.

Book C, page 132. State of N.C. to Darby Calahan 53½ A on S side Matrimony Cr adj sd Callahan, Joshua Hopper. Nov.17,1790.

Book C, page 133. William Collins to William Washington of Caswell Co. adj William Tickle, Watt. Dec. 16, 1788. Joshua Adcock, Stephen Dill.

Book C, page 134. Naman Roberts to Elizabeth Roberts for 15 pds 70 A on N side Dan R adj Sneed Strong land whereon John Menzies lives, land conveyed to my by Sheriff John Hunter Esq which land was sold to satisfy debts of Joseph Roberts dec'd. Jan. 10, 1790. Thomas Henderson, John May, Syrus L. Roberts.

Book C, page 135. Benjamin Cook to Henry Harden for 100 pds 100 A on W side Mayo R adj sd Cook, Andrew Joyce, Sarah Gentry, Elijah Joice. Nov. 10, 1787. John Whitworth, John Brewer, Elizabeth Shackleford.

Book C, page 136. William Plumlee & wife Phebe of Burk Co. to Robert Boak for 600 pds 600 A on both sides Piney Cr adj John Macey, Charles Baker. Jan. 20, 1791. Denton Plumlee, John Boak.

Book C, page 137. Lerkin Peirpoint of Silivan Co. to John Dill for 200 pds 232 A on Wolf Island Cr adj William Self, Bethell, Samuel Watt, Deneal. Aug. 6, 1790. John Billingsly, Moses Allen.

Book C, page 138. Hugh Kirk Patrick of Guilford Co. to James Archer for 5 pds 240 A on Upper Hogans Cr adj James Lomax, John McPeak. May 13, 1791. Thos. Blair, James Hays.

Book C, page 139. William Collins.of Chatham Co. to Thomas Certain of Warren Co. for 25 pds 50 A on Hogans Cr. Nov. 20, 1787. Joshua Adcock, Newton Foote.

Book C, page 140. Thomas King Jr. to Sutton McCollister for 50 pds 200 A on Jacobs Cr adj Joseph Cunningham, James Brown. Mar. 1, 1792. Henry Hendrick, James Brown, Thomas Pound.

Book C, page 141. Andrew Martin to Robert Martin for 150 pds 223 A on both sides Piney Br adj Plumley, Soloman West. Feb. 28, 1792. Walter Martin, Lacy Dollerhide (her mark).

Book C, page 142. Walter Martin to Robert Martin for 150 pds 200 A on N side Piney Cr adj John Mabery, Soloman West, Perkins. land purchased of William Plumbly. Nov. 10, 1791. Joseph Rhodes, Samuel Hernon.

Book C, page 143. Hall Williamson of Caswell Co. to Alexander Pasehal of Caswell Co. for 60 pds 50 A. Jan. 4, 1792. Thomas Key, Thomas Serin.

Book C, page 144. Hall Williamson of Caswell Co. to Joseph Garner for 60 pds 50 A on Cabban Br of Hogans Cr. Nov. 18, 1791. Thomas Chambers, Elisha Dyer, Edmund Jones.

Book C, page 145. John Herron to William Walker for 100 pds 185 A on both sides Little Troublesome Cr. Feb. 28, 1792. Nathaniel Linder, William Walker.

Book C, page 146. Joel Walker to Allen Walker for 60 pds 200 A on S side Dan R adj Joel Walker, Gideon Johnston. Feb. 29,1792.

Book C, page 147. William Johnson & wife Sarah to John Bellenfant for 120 pds 310 A on River bank adj James Ray, George Peay, Covington, Adam Tate. Feb. 15, 1792. George Peay Sr., John May, Thomas Peay.

Book C, page 148. James Grant Sr. & John Grant of Caswell Co. to Drury Yeoman for 1,000 pds Va. money 298 A on Dan R. Feb. 23, 1792. Reuben Grant, Thomas Brooks.

Book C, page 149. Robert Small & wife Elizabeth to Thomas Moore for 90 pds 150 A on both sides Piney Cr adj Charles Baker. May 1, 1789. Jesse McCollister, John Moore.

Book C, page 150. William Mount to Thomas Chambers for 900 pds 240 A on Lickfork of Hogans Cr adj Thomas Miller, John Horsford. Sept. 21, 1790. Wm. McCollum, John Odell, Charles Mitchell.

Book C, page 151. Thomas James & wife Elizabeth (Assignee of William Diamond) to Levy Garrison for 50 pds 100 A on Lickfork of Hogans Cr adj James Hays, David Settle, Moses Garrison. Feb. 23, 1791. Dennis Kelley, John Lain.

Book C, page 152. Thomas Conner to John Conner for 50 pds 250 A on both sides Little Troublesome Cr adj William Walker. Aug. 5, 1791. A. Philips, Nathl. Linder.

Book C, page 153. Thomas Conner to William Conner for 50 pds 250 A on S side Little Troublesome Cr. Aug. 5, 1791. A. Philips, Nathl. Linder.

Book C, page 154. John Odineal & wife Sarah to Wyat Stubblefield for 50 pds 56 A on Wolf Island Cr adj Samuel Watt. Feb. 28, 1792. John Odineal Jr., Richard Stubblefield Jr. John Durham.

Book C, page 155. John Conn to John Sprout for 180 pds 173 A on both sides Big Troublesome Cr adj Thomas Holgan, George Roland, Robert Boak, being land granted to Simon Dunn & sold to sd Conn. May 9, 1792. A. Philips, William Jones, James Sprout.

Book C, page 156. State of N.C. to James Hays 100 A on both sides Jacobs Cr adj John Deavour. Dec. 20, 1791.

Book C, page 157. William Johnson to Charles Galloway & Co. for 90 pds 592 A on N side Dan R on Adams Br. Feb. 28, 1791. M. Hardin Jr., Adam Tate, Hopkins Lacy.

Book C, page 158. John Conn to William Jones Jr. for 142 pds 178 A on S side Big Troublesome Cr adj John Sprout, line of George Roland dec'd. May 5, 1792. A. Philips, John Sprout, Robt. Boak.

Book C, page 159. John Bankson to Robert Cummings for 50 pds 123 A on Troublesome Cr adj James Mulloy (land formerly John Faulkner's), Henry Brewer, line of James Lanier dec'd. Feb. 13, 1788. Isham Lanier, Cynthia Philips.

Book C, page 160. State of N.C. to Levi Garrison 106 A on Vaughan's Cr & Lickfork adj Moses Garrison, Moravian line. Nov. 17, 1790.

Thomas Chambers & wife Phebe to Thomas Mullin Jr. for 900 pds 250 A on N side of Lickfork of Hogans Cr adj sd Mullin. Dec. 1791. David Settle, William Cockril. Ack. in Open Court by W. Tethell as C.C.

Book C, page 162. Alexander Lyall of Surry Co. to Peter Hunter for 30 pds Va. money 92 A on S side Mayo R. Aug. 31, 1790. George Hunter, John Hunter, Thomas Jamison.

Book C, page 163. Notley Jordan & wife Polley to William Russell for 100 pds 200 A on Lickfork of Wolf Island Cr adj Thomas Mullin, Marr, Bethell. April 21, 1792. Lewis Cockrill, John Wright.

Book C, page 164. State of N.C. to William Oldham Short 130 A on Big Troublesome Cr adj Widow Short, Thomas Massey, John Baker, Thomas Henderson. Nov. 17, 1790.

Book C, page 165. State of N.C. to Henry Hendricks 52 A on both sides Little Rockhouse Cr adj David Caldwell, Cornelus Mabery. Nov. 17, 1790.

Book C, page 166. State of N.C. to William Miller 50 A on Gr Rockhouse Cr on the Haw Br adj sd Miller, Benjamin Haggard. Nov. 11, 1790.

Book C, page 167. State of N.C. to Thomas Bernard 45 A on S side Little Rockhouse Cr. Nov. 17, 1790.

Book C, page 168. State of N.C. to Thomas Lomax 50 A on Lickfork of Hogans Cr adj George Brock, Gentry Thomason, Willis Purett. Nov. 17, 1790.

Book C, page 169. John Mecum to Nehemiah Vernon for 20 pds in gold or silver Proclamation money which sd John Mecum is indebted to sd Vernon and for 4 sh pd by sd Vernon 50 A adj Joshua Smith, Jarratt Patterson, Andrew Joyce. June 10, 1791. Jno. Joyce, Thomas Joyce, James Vernon.

Book C, page 170. John Davis to Richard Sharp for 160 pds 280 A on both sides Bever Island Cr adj Charles Perkins, being land granted to Robert Jones Jr., then to Joseph Tate. May 26, 1792. Joshua Smith, William Peay.

Book C, page 171. Mary Lanier, Sampson Lanier & wife Elizabeth Lanier to George Lemonds for 112 pds 180 A on Big Troublesome Cr adj Harston, Marr, Hubbard Peeples, Robert Cummings, Francis McBride, this being part of grant to James Lanier dec'd. Apr. 6, 1792. A. Philips, Robert Cumming, John Lemond.

Book C, page 172. William Southerland to James Strong, John Strong & John Perkins for 180 pds 300 A on both sides Belews Cr adj Stokes Co., Nelson, this being tract taken up by John Southerland. May 26, 1792.

Book C, page 173. David Alexander to Jones Parish for 50 pds 100 A on N fork Buffalow Island Cr. Dec. 28, 1791. John Parish, Cager Hill.

Book C, page 174. Laurance Bankson to Isaac Cantrell for 50 pds 100 A on Wolf Island Cr. 1792. A. Philips, Robert Brown.

Book C, page 175. David Peeples of Green Co., Ga. to William Pratt for 100 pds 300 A on a br of Jacobs Cr. Nov. 14, 1791. Nathan Massey, Henry Lanier, Hubbard Peeples.

Book C, page 176. State of N.C. to Nathaniel Linder, Assignee of John Hayns 100 A adj Robert Walker, Charles Mitchell, Isaac Philips. Nov. 17, 1790.

Book C, page 177. State of N.C. to Zackariah Robinson 100 A on Hazel Br of Gr Rockhouse Cr. Nov. 8, 1784.

Book C, page 178. State of N.C. to John Pritchet 26 A on Haw R adj his father, George Dilworth, Francis Hodge, John Hayes. Nov. 17, 1790.

Book C, page 179. John Hays to John Lewis for 50 pds 131 A on N side Haw R adj Widdow Boyd, Pritchet, also 69 A granted to James Nichols by Granville on Haw R. May 19, 1792. Thomas North, John Dilworth, James Nickell.

Book C, page 180. Elisha Briggs & wife Margaret to Samuel Hill for 25 pds 220 A adj John Donnel. May 9, 1792. A. Boyd, Jane Wilson.

Book C, page 181. State of N.C. to Andrew Martin 400 A on both sides Rockey Br of Big Troublesome Cr adj Robert Boak, Soloman Webster, Mathew George. Dec. 20, 1791.

Book C, page 182. State of N.C. to Robert Boak 137 A on Troublesome Cr adj Widow West, Hugh Linch, William Jones, Andrew Martin. Nov. 17, 1790.

Book C, page 183. Minos Cannon of Randolph Co. to Joseph Lemonds for 15 pds 150 A in Davidson Co. on Mill Cr & Stow R at N edge of Big Hurricane adj sd Cannon. Jan. 13, 1792. John Rowland, John Lemond.

Book C, page 184. Isaac James & William James of Laurence Co., S.C. to Nathaniel Harris for 50 pds Va. money 100 A on Matrimony Cr, being land that Abraham James settled his son Isaac on, adj Abraham James. Oct. 11, 1786. Archer Murphey, Jesse Harris.

Book C, page 185. William Bethell to Thomas North for 50 pds 50 A on Wolf Island Cr adj Richard Marr, Dicks Road. Jan. 28, 1792. Ack. in Court by William Bethell C. C.

Book C, page 186. State of N.C. to Joshua Allen for 594 A on S side Hogans Cr adj George Allen, Nathaniel Williams, John Dennis, John Herrin, Peter Oneal, William Clark. Nov. 17, 1790.

Book C, page 187. State of N.C. to John Horford Taylor 296 A on Lickfork adj Hugh Reed (formerly Jacob Williams), Edward Taylor, John Harris, Josiah Hancock. Dec. 20, 1791.

Book C, page 188. State of N.C. to John Stockard 50 A on both sides Rockey fork of Jacobs Cr. Dec. 20, 1791.

Book C, page 189. State of N.C. to Thomas King Sr. 100 A on Gr Troublesome Cr adj Alexander Brown, Moses Short, Thomas Massey. Dec. 20, 1791.

Book C, page 190. State of N.C. to William Oldham Short 40 A on Jacobs Cr. Dec. 20, 1791.

Book C, page 191. State of N.C. to William Oldham Short 100 A on both sides Jacobs Cr adj Zaza Brasher, Patrick Mullin. Dec. 20, 1791.

Book C, page 192. State of N.C. to George Brown 100 A on Trouble-some Cr adj John D. Carner. Dec. 20, 1791.

Book C, page 194. State of N.C. to John Pound 50 A on Wolf Is-land Cr adj Jacob Cantrill, Elisha Barnard, Jacob Bernard. Dec. 20, 1791.

Book C, page 195. State of N.C. to Aaron Allen 150 A on Brushey fork of Gr Rockhouse Cr adj Job Baker, William Jones, Joseph Cunningham. Dec. 20, 1791.

Book C, page 196. State of N.C. to Aaron Allen 195 A on Big Rockhouse Cr adj James Brown, William Baker, James McCarrol, David Pursel, John Young. Dec. 20, 1791.

Book C, page 197. George Bruce of Caswell Co. to William Harri-son for 50 pds 250 A on both sides Little Wolf Island Cr adj John Gunter, John Simmons, William Trainum, being land granted to Thomas Bruce. Mar. 12, 1792. Richd. Marr, James McCubbin, John Odell.

Book C, page 198. Ezekiel Calahan to Henry Grogan for 40 pds Va. money 100 A on Poplar Br of Matrimony Cr. Feb. 16, 1791. Mainyard Colley, Moses Lord.

Book C, page 199. Nathaniel Linder to George Rolands for 50 pds 100 A on Gr Rockhouse Cr adj Robert Walker, Charles Mitchell, Isaac Philips. Sept. 20, 1792. A. Philips, John Stanford, Robert Boak.

Book C, page 200. John Matlock to Joseph Philips for 50 pds 111 A on Hogans Cr adj Clark, Thacker, Samuel Watt. Aug. 1792.

Book C, page 201. Thomas Parks of Lawrance Co., S.C. to Bryant Senior (also spelled Seanor) for 200 pds 160 A on E side Hogans Cr adj Dean. Oct. 16, 1792. Joel Dean, Cornelus Davis.

Book C, page 202. Walter Hill to Thomas Scott for 10 pds 15 A on Benajah Cr adj sd Scott, Charles Bruce. Nov. 29, 1790. A. Philips, Edward Williams, Robert Boak.

Book C, page 203. William Taylor to Gentry Thompson for 30 pds 100 A adj John Thomson, Aaron Arnold, William Overbey's line (land now bel to sd Taylor), Widdow Savage. 1788. Wm. Hubbart, James Owen, Easter Hubbart.

Book C, page 204. Andrew Martin to Walter Martin for a certain sum 268 A on Big Troublesome Stoney Br adj Mathew George, Robert Boak, Wm. Jones, being tract on which Walter Martin lives & part of tract on which I live. Nov. 6, 1792.

Book C, page 205. Isaac Connoly to William Stratton for 120 pds 320 A on Little Troublesome Cr adj James Nickol. Sept. 15, 1792. John Sprout, James Sprout.

Book C, page 206. John Linder to John Smith for 10 pds 200 A on Wolf Island Cr adj Martin, Browder. Sept. 6, 1792. Samuel Smith, Martha Smith.

Book C, page 207. Richard Roberts to George Kimble for 150 pds Va. curr. 194 A on N side Dan R on both sides Matrimony Cr adj Va. line, Christopher Cobler. Dec. 9, 1790. Joseph Hopper, Jesse Hinton, Thomas A. Roberts.

Book C, page 208. Charles Bruce of Guilford Co. to Thomas Simpson of Guilford Co. for 25 pds actual gold & silver 150 A on Bear Br adj Samuel Short. June 12, 1792. Edw. Richardson, Richard Simpson Jr.

Book C, page 209. Lawrence Bankson to John Linder for 100 pds 150 A on Mills Cr adj Widow Browder, Isaac Cantrell. Dec. 29, 1791. John Mitchell, James Mitchell.

Book C, page 210. Thomas Allen to David Peeples for 200 pds 300 A on Jacobs Cr adj sd Peeples. Aug. 22, 1786. Nathl. Lanier, Nathl. Peebles, Hubbard Peebles.

Book C, page 211. John Simmons to Joseph McGloban of Va. for 30 pds 100 A tract whereon Isham Simmons lives, on Piney fork of Town Cr. Nov. 28, 1791. John Brochus, Thomas Brown, John Odineal.

Book C, page 212. John Simmons & wife Elizabeth to Robert Lilley for 20 pds 100 A on both sides N prong of Piney fork of Town Cr. May 7, 1792. Joseph McGloughlen, John Armstrong.

Book C, page 213. John Bankson to Laurance Bankson for 60 pds
300 A on Wolf Island Cr adj Widow Browder, Charles Harris, Nathaniel Newman, Isaac Cantrell, John Linder. Dec. 9, 1790. John
Linder, John Cantrell.

Book C, page 214. Soloman Webster to Moses Dean for 20 pds 50 A
on Little Troublesome Cr. 1792.

Book C, page 215. Thomas Lomax to William Stapleton for 20 pds
50 A on Lickfork of Hogans Cr adj George Brock, Gentry Thompson,
Willis Pruet. Aug. 27, 1792. John Horford Taylor, Daniel Atkins.

Book C, page 216. Nicholas McCubbin to William Bloyd for 150
pds Va. money 238 A on both sides London Cr of Wolf Island Cr
adj Mark London, William Stubblefield. Aug. 27, 1792. Richd.
Marr, William Traynem, John Bloyd.

Book C, page 217. State of N.C. to Gideon Vaughan 100 A on
Pruits fork of Hogans Cr adj Thomas Williams, David Vaughan,
Samuel Watts. Nov. 17, 1790.

Book C, page 218. Mathew George to Duncan Beith for 78 pds 12
sh 131 A on Big Troublesome Cr adj Walter Martin. Nov. 13, 1792.
A. Philips, William McCleroy, Solomon Webster.

Book C, page 219. John Pratt to Richard Pratt for 16 pds 27 A
on Sharps Cr of Dan R adj sd Richard Pratt, Charles Galloway.
Nov. 15, 1792. John Menzies, Joshua Smith, James Galloway.

Book C, page 220. Batte Cocke Lacy to Theophelus Lacy for 180
pds Va. money 248 A on W side Bever Island Cr. Nov. 6, 1792.
Sam. Henderson, R. Martin, Valentine Allen Jr.

Book C, page 221. Robert Hairis to William Bethell for 20 pds
20 A on both sides Harrises Cr a fork of Hogans Cr being land
granted to Thompson Harris dec'd. Oct. 20, 1792. Richd. Bethell,
Joseph Payne Jr.

Book C, page 222. William Washington to Thomas Key for 130 pds
150 A adj William Tickel. Dec. 27, 1788. Sherwood Nance, Benjamin Cockrean.

Book C, page 223. John Harper to Jesse Hinton for 20 pds 35 A
on Little Buffalow Cr. Feb. 26, 1793. Nathl. Linder, Nathaniel
Tatum, Robert Small.

Book C, page 224. John Leak Esq to Joseph Parks for 50 pds 102
A on Matrimony Cr adj sd Leak, Reece Price. Feb. 26, 1793.

Book C, page 225. John Harper to Joseph Hopper for 20 pds 50 A
on Little Buffalo Cr. Feb. 26, 1793. Nathl Linder, Nathaniel
Tatum, Robert Small. Ack. May 23, 1793 by Joseph Clark.

Book C, page 226. William James to John Harper for 50 pds 400
A on Little Buffalow of Matrimony Cr adj Christopher Coblar,
Richard Roberts, Joseph Hopper. Nov. 27, 1785. Nath. Harris,
Henry Grogan.

Book C, page 227. Ralph Shaw of Stokes Co. to John Shelton for 70 pds 150 A adj Asa Brasher, Peter Mitchell. Apr. 15, 1792. Elijah Shelton, Joseph Arnett.

Book C, page 228. Selathem Newnam to John Harper for 50 pds 100 A on Little Troublesome Cr. Feb. 23, 1793. Shiveral Garner, Edward Newnam.

Book C, page 229. Turbyfield Barnes to Charles Galloway & Co. for 40 pds 150 A. Feb.9,1793. T. Wilson, Edm Burton, John Minzies.

Book C, page 230. Turbafield Barns to Charles Galloway & Co. for 600 pds Va. money 903 A on N fork of Sharps Cr adj Valentine Allen Sr., William H. Allen Jr. Feb.9,1792. T.Wilson Jr., Edm Burton, John Minzies.

Book C, page 232. David Poyner of Caswell Co. to Edward Newnam for 50 pds 100 A on Wolf Island Cr adj William Gorden, Abraham Philips, part of grant to William Spears. May 29, 1791. Shiveral Garner, David McCollum.

Book C, page 233. Robert Payne of Pittsylvania Co., Va. to William Douglas of Rowan Co. for 150 pds Va. money 240 A on Wolf Island Cr adj Caswell Co. line. Jan.12,1793. William Moss, James Clemens.

Book C, page 234. Joseph McCullough to William Walker for 120 pds 240 A on Little Troublesome Cr adj Reuben Lowe. Feb. 6, 1793. A. Philips, John Herron.

Book C, page 235. Isaac Dorris of Orange Co. to Samuel Bethell for 30 pds 200 A on Lickfork of Hogans Cr adj William Bethell, Thomas Mullin. Dec. 15, 1792. Dan Burford, Lewis Barton, Thomas Mullin.

Book C, page 236. Isaac Dorris & wife Susannah of Orange Co. to Thomas Mullins Jr. for 200 pds 200 A on N side Hogans Cr adj sd Mullin. Dec. 15, 1792. Danl. Burford, Lewis Barton, Samuel Bethell.

Book C, page 237. State of N.C. to William Russell 100 A on Wolf Island Cr adj John Linder. Dec. 20, 1791.

Book C, page 238. State of N.C. to William Russell 225¼ A adj sd Russell. Dec. 20, 1791.

Book C, page 239. State of N.C. to William Russell 100 A on Wolf Island Cr adj John Linder. Dec. 20, 1791.

Book C, page 240. State of N.C. to Abraham Philips 28 A on Haw R adj William Robertson, James Higgins, William Bourk, Harris. Dec. 20, 1791.

Book C, page 241. State of N.C. to Almon Guinn 97 A on Blewes Cr adj own line, John Daring, William Watson, Francis Ford. Dec. 20, 1791.

Book C, page 242. State of N.C. to John Jones 50 A on Little Rockhouse Cr adj sd Jones. Dec. 20, 1791.

Book C, page 243. State of N.C. to John Jones 108 A on Little Rockhouse Cr adj sd Jones, Mary Elliott, John McKinney, Cornelus Mabery. Dec. 20, 1791.

Book C, page 245. State of N.C. to Ralph Norris 150 A on both sides Rockey Br. May 16, 1787.

Book C, page 246. State of N.C. to John Stanford 65 A on Big Troublesome Cr adj sd Stanford, William Buckanon. Dec.20,1791.

Book C, page 247. Daniel Allen Jr. to John Allen Jr. for 50 pds 103½ A on a br of Hogans Cr adj Joshua Allen. Mar. 13, 1793. David Settle, Moses Garrison.

Book C, page 248. John Wimbush of Pittsylvania Co., Va. to James Hunter for 250 pds Va. money 630 A on N fork of Bever Island Cr adj Joseph Tate. Sept.9, 1792. James Henderson, Samuel Todd.

Book C, page 249. John Rhodes to James Rigby of Wake Co. for 35 pds 50 A on N side Haw R, adj sd Rhodes. May 7, 1793. Samuel Rhodes, John Warner.

Book C, page 250. Moses Short to William Oldham Short for 160 pds 169 A on both sides Gr Troublesome Cr adj Thomas Green, Stephen Mitchel. Dec.15,1792. George Simon, John Low, John Stockard.

Book C, page 251. Batte C. Lacy to John Lacy for 30 pds Va. money his share in the grant of 437 A to Batte C. Lacy, Hopkins Lacy, Theophelus Lacy, John Lacy & William Lacy on both sides Dan R adj Nicholas Larimore. Nov.10,1792. Phil. Irion, Joshua Smith, Robt. Goins.

Book C, page 252. Batte C. Lacy to John Lacy for 50 pds Va. money 64 A on S side Dan R. Nov. 10, 1792. Joshua Smith, Robt. Goins, Phil. Irion.

Book C, page 253. John Lovill of Greenville Co., S.C. to David Lovell for 200 pds 349 A on both sides Town Cr adj William Hunt, Farguson, Robert Hutson. Dec. 2, 1793. Thos. Cantrell, Thos. Lovell, David Lovell.

Book C, page 254. John Marr to James Frost for 39 pad 39 A on Big Troublesome Cr adj sd Frost. May 29, 1793.

Book C, page 255. James Frost to John Marr for 39 pds 39 A on Big Troublesome Cr adj Marr's Mill Tract, John Stanford. May 29, 1793.

Book C, page 256. Francis McBride to Isaih McBride for 110 pds 340 A on N side Big Troublesome Cr adj Richard Henderson, Philips. Aug. 7, 1792. Samuel McBride, John McBride.

Book C, page 257. State of N.C. to Joel McKey 300 A on Bever Island Cr adj Richard Cardwell, Means, Abraham Martin. May 16, 1787.

Book C, page 258. James Thomson & wife Allis to William Kelley for 100 pds 200 A on Hogans Cr adj John Dilworth, James Walker, being a grant to Jean Dilworth in 1784. Jan. 1793. John Graham, Francis Hodge.

Book C, page 259. Christopher Dudley & wife Frances to Thomas Skinner for 50 pds 60 A on Wolf Island Cr adj John Odineal, Mills. May 23, 1791. Richd Marr, Joseph Newcomb, John Odell.

Book C, page 260. John Hampton of Stokes Co. to Sneed Strong for 40 pds 120 A on N side Gr Whetstone Cr adj sd Hampton, James Galloway, John Loman. Mar.11,1790. Philip Rose, Ebenezar Crumpton.

Book C, page 261. Samuel Finley to Mathew Peggs for 120 pds pd by John Jones 200 A on S fork of Upper Hogans Cr adj Michael Thomas. Mar.10,1791. L. Brory Fare, Crozear Craigg.

Book C, page 262. Stephen Sephew to John Abbit for 100 pds 232 A on both sides Little Rockhouse Cr adj Charles Galloway, Mary Elliott. Aug.26,1790. A. Philips, James Hays Jr., John Jones.

Book C, page 263. David Peeples of Green Co., Ga. to Asa Brasher of Guilford Co. for 100 pds 50 A on both sides Troublesome Cr, Samuel Young, Moses Campbell, David Peeples' mill pond. Jan. 3, 1793. Charles Bruce, Thomas Massey, Burrel Peeples.

Book C, page 264. Alexander Lyall & John Hunter to George Hunter for 20 pds a tract on N side Mayo R at mouth of small br, adj sd Hunter, William Motley. Aug.6,1791. James Kelley, Richard Martin.

Book C, page 265. Sarah Williams, Alexander Lyalls, Abraham Mayes, Joseph Williams, John Williams, Elisha Williams, John Vaughters and James McCommack of Ga. to John Hunter for 40 pds a tract on S side Mayo R. Sept. 3, 1790. Wm. Motley, Peter Hunter, Umphry Broockes, George Hunter.

Book C, page 266. Sarah Williams, Alexander Lyall, Abram Mayes, Joseph Williams, John Williams, Elisha Williams all of Rocking-ham and James McCommack of Ga. to John Hunter for 50 pds a tract on N side Mayo R adj sd Lyall. Sept. 3, 1790. Wm. McColley, Peter Hunter, Umphy Broackes, George Hunter.

Book C, page 267. William Young to Benjamin Williams for 10 pds 45 A on Wolf Island Cr adj Thomas King. Feb. 23, 1790. A. Philips, Nathl. Linder, Allen Williams.

Book C, page 268. Reuben Jackson to James Jackson for 50 pds 50 A on Mayo R. Oct. 24, 1789. Robert Means, William Motley, She-sley Barnes.

Book C, page 269. Henry Chambless to John Simmons Jr. for 100 pds 200 A on Town Cr adj Samuel Denton, David Lovell, William Hubbard. Sept. 19, 1789. Henry Martin, John Norris.

Book C, page 270. Joshua Mabry & Joel Gibson to William Callom for 30 pds 220 A adj land of Mabry & Gibson. Jan. 23, 1787. Wm. Motley, Spencer Callom.

Book C, page 271. Alexander McClaran for 50 pds 100 A on S side Dan R adj William Johnson, William Astin, Gideon Johnson. Nov. 29, 1791. Joshua Smith, John Bradley.

Book C, page 272. Nathaniel Paris to John Moore for 20 pds land on both sides Camp Br of Gr Troublesome Cr adj Iron Works, James McCleland. Nov. 28, 1791. Francis McBride, John McBride.

Book C, page 273. John McCarrell to Thomas Faulkner for 50 pds 60 A on Pinia Br. Oct. 13, 1792. John Mackey, Bachel Vermilion.

Book C, page 274. Nancy McAlroy to William McAlroy for 50 pds 348 A on S side Haw R adj James S. McAlroy, Edward Richardson, James Craiton being part of 2 tracts granted to George Martin. Nov. 30, 1792. T. Curry, Nathan Guerin, A. Philips, Richard Hopkins.

Book C, page 275. State of N.C. to Guy Vermilion 3 A on Little Troublesome Cr & Piney Cr adj sd Vermilion, William Harrison, John McCarrell. Dec. 20, 1791.

Book C, page 276. State of N.C. to Andrew Martin 142 A on both sides Rockey fork of Big Troublesome Cr adj own line, Robert Boak. Dec. 20, 1791.

Book C, page 277. State of N.C. to John Covinton 117 A on Wolf Island & Troublesome Crs adj Patrick Wardlow, Robert Martin, Abraham Philips, John Hanes. Dec. 20, 1791.

Book C, page 278. State of N.C. to Ezekiel Wright 62½ A on Jacobs Cr adj sd Wright, William Jones, Nathaniel Linder. Dec. 20, 1791.

Book C, page 279. State of N.C. to John Marr Assignee for Peter Perkins 100 A on both sides Wolf Island Cr adj John Odineal, Widow Fletcher. Nov. 17, 1790.

Book C, page 280. State of N.C. to George Hairston & John Marr, Assignees for William Trammill, 118 A on Haw R & Troublesome Cr adj William Leamon, Jonas Frost, James Barnes. Nov. 17, 1790.

Book C, page 281. State of N.C. to Joseph Payne 44 A on Troublesome Cr adj John Allen, John Herring. Dec. 20, 1791.

Book C, page 282. State of N.C. to James Walker 49 A on Hogans Cr. adj Joseph Payne, Alexander Walker, Thomas Dilworth. Dec. 20, 1791.

Book C, page 283. State of N.C. to Elijah Brown 120 A on Hogans Cr adj James Gill, Charles Dean, Caswell Co. line. Dec.20,1791.

Book C, page 284. State of N.C. to James Hodge 200 A on Hogans Cr adj Samuel Watt, Joshua Wright. Dec. 20, 1791.

Book C, page 285. State of N.C. to Zaza Brasher 100 A on Jacobs Cr adj Moxley, Patrick Mullen. July 11, 1788.

Book C, page 286. State of N.C. to Jacob Cantrill 200 A on Wolf Island Cr adj sd Cantrill, John Granger, Isaac Cantrell, Bankson. July 11, 1788.

Book C, page 287. State of N.C. to Richard Vernon 100 A on Mountain Run Cr adj William Lewis. Oct. 22, 1782.

Book C, page 288. State of N.C. to Moses Barrow 250 A on both sides Kirbys Cr. Nov. 17, 1790.

Book C, page 289. State of N.C. to John Fargison 66 A on Dan R adj Peter Stephens, Moses Barrow. Nov. 17, 1790.

Book C, page 290. John Humphreys & wife Elizabeth to John Watt for 100 pds 82 A on Hogans Cr adj Samuel Watt, Charles Dean, being land purchased from William Bethell. Aug. 13, 1791. William Barker, Ezekel Jones.

Book C, page 291. Daniel Allen Jr. to Daniel Allen Sr. for 50 pds 100 A on Hogans Cr adj own lines. Mar. 13, 1793. David Settle, Moses Garrison.

Book C, page 292. Soloman Allen to Samuel Allen for 50 pds 100 A on Hogans Cr adj Samuel Watt. Jan. 20, 1792. David Settle, Joseph Clark.

Book C, page 293. William Hubbert to David Settle for 100 pds 40 A on Lickfork of Hogans Cr adj Moses Garrison, Moravian line. Mar. 13, 1793. John Allen, Daniel Allen.

Book C, page 294. Soloman Allen to Samuel Watt Jr. for 50 pds 25 A on Hogans Cr adj sd Watt, Charles Deen. Apr. 13, 1792. Elisha Dyer, Baldy Dyer.

Book C, page 295. Edward Scott & wife Sarah to Soloman Allen for 200 pds 200 A on S side Hogans Cr adj Samuel Watt, Charles Dean. Apr. 1, 1791. Samuel Watt, Samuel Allen, Elijah Brown.

Book C, page 296. Alexander Joyce, High Sherriff, to Adam Tate Esq for 109 pds 450 A on Wolf Island Cr adj Archibald Yarbrough, William Bethell, Fletcher, this being land seized for payment of debt of estate of John Odineal dec'd on order from Guilford Co. Court. Jan. 30, 1793.

Book C, page 297. Abraham Philips to William Roberson for $23 28 A on Haw R adj James Higgins, William Bourk, Harris. Mar. 27, 1793. John Roberson, Will. Bethell.

Book C, page 298. Alexander Joyce, High Sheriff to William Pritchet for 150 pds land adj Thomas Hays, Joel Johnson, John Cunningham, this being land seized and sold to highest bidder to pay debt of estate of James Jeremiah Pritchett, William Bethell.

Book C, page 299. Lawrence Bankson & wife Sarah to Letitha Browder for 100 pds Va. curr 100 A on N side Wolf Island Cr. & Mill Cr adj John Linder. Aug.10,1785. John Linder, Charles Gilley.

Book C, page 300. John Odineal to Wyat Stubblefield of Caswell Co. for 70 pds pd by John Marr to Isaac Clark, Sheriff, to satisfy execution against estate of John Odineal, 240 A on E side Wolf Island Cr. Mar.4,1791. Drury Smith, John Odineal Jr., Thomas Hatfield.

Book C, page 301. Peter Oneal to James Taylor for 150 pds 100 A on Hogans Cr adj Clark. Jan. 12, 1790.

Book C, page 302. Isaac Clark Esq, Sheriff, to Thomas Green, Assignee of John Marr for 12 pds 153 A on both sides Troublesome Cr adj Moses Short, this being land of Aron Short seized to satisfy debt to William Mebane. May 25, 1793. Joseph Clark.

Book C, page 303. Thomas Green of Stokes Co. to William Oldham Short for 10 pds 42 A on N side Big Troublesome Cr adj Thomas Massey. July 31, 1793. Thomas Lomax, Moses Lomax, Elizabeth Lomax.

Book C, page 304. John Chadwell to William Astin for 170 pds 200 A on S side Dan R adj sd Astin; also 102 A on Cokers Cr adj Alexander Martin, Philemon Gates; also 4 A on both sides Dan R including an island. Aug. 28, 1793. W. Bethell.

Book C, page 305. Turbafield Barns to William Hunt Allen for 10 pds 32½ A on both sides Buckhorn Br of Dan R adj Richard Sharp, Vaul Allen. May 29, 1793. A. Philips, John Menzies.

Book C, page 306. Jacob Cantrell to Isaac Cantrell for 24 pds 100 A on Wolf Island Cr adj Bankson, Wardlow. Aug. 27, 1793. Henry Hendricks, Elisha Bernard.

Book C, page 307. State of N.C. to Henry Colson 100 A on N side Bever Island Cr on both sides Rich Bottom Br adj John Joyce, James Hunter. Dec. 20, 1791.

Book C, page 308. State of N.C. to John Smith 250 A on Quac Quaw Cr adj Lawrance Porter. Dec. 20, 1791.

Book C, page 309. John Horford Taylor to James Saunders for 1,000 lbs. tobacco 96 A on Lickfork of Hogans Cr. Feb. 26, 1793. Daniel Atkins, John Cantrell.

Book C, page 310. Nicholas Larrimore to Hance Larrimore for 200 pds 640 A on both sides Jeffs Cr adj Robert Goins. Sept. 30, 1792. John Philips, Wm. McClellen, Saml. Larimore.

Book C, page 311. James Jackson to Nathan Oakey for 20 pds 100 A on Buffalo Cr adj Stokes Co. line. Apr. 20, 1793. William Martin, Young Gill, John Steward.

Book C, page 312. William Tranam & wife Sarah to John Payne for 100 pds 200 A on Wolf Island Cr. Feb. 7, 1793. Lawrance Porter, Coloson Porter, William McCollum.

Book C, page 313. Cornelus Cook to John Warren of Guilford Co. for 100 pds 100 A on Wrights fork of Belews Cr adj James More. Jan. 1, 1793. Constantine Ladd, Henry Cook, Mary Ladd.

Book C, page 314. William Pritchet & wife Margaret to James Smith for 500 pds 105 A on Haw R adj Cunningham. Aug. 26, 1793. Thomas Spencer, James Mateer, Wm. Pritchett.

Book C, page 315. Benjamin Bowen of Pendleman Co., S.C. to John Warren of Guilford Co. for 50 pds 300 A on W fork of Upper Hogans Cr adj Thomas Bowen. Dec. 29, 1792. John McPeak, John Hollowday, John Lovel.

Book C, page 316. Thomas Scott to John Wafford for 20 pds 40 A on Benajah Cr adj Rowland. Aug. 28, 1793. A. Philips, Elijah Hains.

Book C, page 317. John Waford to Michael Caffey for 31 pds 62 A on Big Troublesome Cr adj sd Caffey, Thomas Holgan, James Johnson. Aug. 24, 1793.

Book C, page 318. Alexander Joyce, High Sheriff to William Clark for 62 pds a negro woman slave sold at auction to highest bidder to satisfy debt of Peter Oneal directed by William Bethell, Clerk of Court. Feb. 27, 1792. A. Philips, Rich. Bethell.

Book C, page 319. Nelson Fields & wife Mary and Mary Fields Sr. and Allen Fields to Elisha Joyce for 300 pds 160 A on Mountain Run adj sd Joyce, Mary Fields, Joshua Smith, John Fields. Nov. 27, 1792. Robert Joyce, William Fields, Ariel Fields.

Book C, page 320. State of N.C. to John Price 125 A on S fork of Stewarts Cr. Dec. 20, 1791.

Book C, page 321. Abraham Philips to James Webster for 30 pds 60 A on Little Troublesome Cr adj Henry Goins, Bailey Martin. Sept. 3, 1793. Robt Boak, Jeremiah West.

Book C, page 322. Asa Brasher to Thomas Knight for 30 pds 140 A on N side Jacobs Cr. July 2, 1791. John Stockird, John McPeak.

Book C, page 323. Solomon Webster to John Webster for 40 pds 100 A on both Troublesome Crs adj John Hayns, Jesse Broughton, being tract granted to Hugh Harkins & sold to Soloman Webster. 179_.

Book C, page 324. Francis McBride to Isaiah McBride for 50 pds 60½ A on Troublesome Cr adj Richard Henderson. Jan. 21, 1793. A. Philips, Asa McBride, John McBride.

Book C, page 325. Benjamin Spencer to Daniel Allen for 100 pds in Gold & Silver 3 negroes. Oct. 22, 1793. Joseph Clark.

Book C, page 325. Nathaniel Williams to Alexander Joyce for 50 pds a negro girl Cloe & a boy Thomas. Mar.16,1793. Isaac Clark, N. Williams.

Book C, page 326. William Pritchet to John Spencer of Caswell Co. for 100 pds 96 A on S side Haw R adj John Cunningham. Feb. 12, 1793. Benjn. Spencer, Jeremiah Pritchet.

Book C, page 327. Nathaniel Linder to William Miller for 30 pds 50 A on Jacobs Cr adj Richard Hingson, William Hubbard, William Craigg, being part of grant to Adam Baker & sold to sd Linder. Nov. 26, 1793. A. Philips, Richd. Marr.

Book C, page 328. Thomas Bernard to Twerangon Butt for 10 pds 37 A on both sides Little Rockhouse Cr adj sd Butt, Widow Overbey, being land bought of John Morton. Nov. 15, 1793. A. Philips, Anne Booker Bernard.

Book C, page 329. Isaiah McBride to John McBride for 50 pds 50 A on Gr Troublesome Cr. Jan. 21, 1793. A. Philips, Jos. McBride, Wm. Leekey.

Book C, page 330. Nathaniel Linder to Richard Hingson for 50 pds 100 A on Jacobs Cr adj William Hubbart. Nov. 26, 1793. A. Philips, John Stockard.

Book C, page 331. Henry Hardin of Wilks Co., Ga. to Mark Hardin for 100 pds 200 A on both sides Beaver Island Cr of Dan R. Oct. 12, 1793. Sam Henderson, Doshea Callaway, Fanny Henderson.

Book C, page 332. John Gibson to Reece Price for 100 pds 265 A on Middle Fork of Buffalow Island Cr adj Joseph Odel. Nov. 26, 1793. John May, John Fields.

Book C, page 333. Reece Price to John Gibson for 100 pds 100 A on both sides Matrimony Cr adj James Leak. Nov. 26, 1793. John May, John Whitworth.

Book C, page 334. Reece Price to John Gibson for 150 pds 165 A adj John Leak, Farley. Nov. 26, 1793. John May, John Fields.

Book C, page 335. John Oliver to Peter Oliver for 50 pds 50 A adj James Oliver, Robert Gilleland. July 13, 1793. Philip Gates, James Oliver.

Book C, page 336. John Oliver to James Oliver for 50 pds 100 A on S side Hogans Cr adj Joseph Gates. July 13, 1793. Philip Gates, Peter Oliver.

Book C, page 337. Anthony Dearing of Stokes Co. to William Crump for 100 pds 300 A on Beaver Island Cr adj sd Crump, Surry Co. line. Nov. 27, 1793. W. Bethell.

Book C, page 338. William McKinsey to John Holladay for 100 pds 100 A on both sides Hogan Cr adj Michael Thomas, being tract conveyed to John Cummins by Sheriff John May. Dec. 14, 1792. John Love, Fargus Moor.

Book C, page 339. John Hunter to Andrew Hunter for 20 pds Va. money 160 A on S side Mayo R adj James Brison. Aug. 31, 1793. William Motley, George Hunter, Joseph Jenkins.

Book C, page 340. Benjamin Cook to William Crunk Jennings for 110 pds 260 A on Shepherds Cr of Mayo R adj Henry Harding, Peter Harston. Nov. 23, 1791. Joshua Smith, Richard Bondurant, John Joyce.

Book C, page 341. Benjamin Cook to William Crunk Jennings for 10 pds 200 A on Shepherds Cr adj Elijah Joyce. Nov. 23, 1791. Joshua Smith, Richard Bondurant, John Joyce.

Book C, page 342. State of N.C. to Alem B. Williams, Assignee for William Clark, 150 A on both sides Town Cr adj sd Williams, Thomas Raffety, Leaven Mitchel. Nov. 17, 1790.

Book C, page 343. State of N.C. to William Buckanon 300 A on both sides Troublesome Cr adj Mary Patrick. Nov. 27, 1792.

Book C, page 344. State of N.C. to William Buckanon 400 A on Haw R adj Mary Patrick. Nov. 27, 1792.

Book C, page 345. William Bethell to John Johnson for 50 pds 35 A on Lickfork of Hagans Cr adj Thomas Mullen. Sept. 20, 1788. Samuel Bethell, Mary Walker, Richard Bethell.

Book C, page 346.   Allen West to Walter Martin for 49 pds 72 A on
Rockey fork of Troublesome Cr adj sd Martin, Soloman West, James
West, Robert Martin.   Sept. 16, 1793.   J. Waford, Jeremiah West.

Book C, page 347.   John McCollum to James McCollum for 50 pds Va.
money 166 A on Hogans Cr being part of tract granted to Daniel
McCollum dec'd.   Feb. 8, 1794.   W. Bethell, John Thrasher,
William McCollum.

Book C, page 348.   John McCollum Sr. of Caswell Co. to Isaac
McCollum, Jacob McCollum, Thrasher McCollum, Cloud McCollum for
60 pds 389 A on N side Hogans Cr adj William Bethell.   Feb. 8,
1794.   W. Bethell, John Thrasher, William McCollum.

Book C, page 349.   Drury Yeoman to Shadrich Yeoman for 400 pds
100 A known as Blairs Bent whereon Drury Yeoman dec'd lived on
Buck Shoals of Dan R adj the Wagon Road, George Peay.   Feb. 25,
1794.   William Clark, R. Eastham.

Book C, page 350.   Robert Russell of Guilford Co. to Edward
Weatherly for 100 pds 300 A on Haw R adj Thomas Rese, William
Case, Stephen Mitchel, Marr, Thomas More, Charles More, land
being granted in 1783 to Richard Lovell, sold to Hezekiah Rhoads
and then to sd Russell.   Feb. 12, 1794.   Edward Weatherly,
Martin Weatherly, John Weatherly.

Book C, page 351.   John Fendel Carr & wife Elizabeth to Zachariah
King for & in a valuable consideration 300 A on S side Mayo R
adj William Mills being a new line drawn by Henry Burch and
Reuben Jackson crossing Buffalo Cr adj Reuben Jackson, William
Moore.   Nov. 29, 1792.   James Jackson, Thomas Jackson, Chesley
Barnes.

BOOK D

Book D, page 1.   State of N.C. to Adam Trolinger 106 A on Rockey
fork of Jacobs Cr adj Nathaniel Linder, John Stockard, Alexander
Martin, Esq.   June 27, 1793.

Book D, page 2.   State of N.C. to Thomas Raffety 75 A on Town Cr
adj Allem B. Williams.   Dec. 20, 1791.

Book D, page 3.   Alexander Joyce Esq., High Sheriff to Charles
Moore for 30 pds as highest bidder of 37 A seized and put up for
sale for debt against estate of James Mulloy dec'd, which sd sum
was paid to Charles Bruce, Commissioner of Confiscated Property
of Guilford Co.   Jan. 21, 1794.   Peter Watson, Drury Williams.

Book D, page 4.   John Linder to John Martin for 20 pds 200 A on
both sides Gumping Br adj sd Linder, Browder.   Aug. 7, 1793.
John Cantrill, Sampson (or Tompson?) Cantrell.

Book D, page 6.   John London to Henry Wall for 10 sh 150 A on N
side Stones fork of Wolf Island Cr adj John McCubbin.   Dec. 3,
1793.   Thomas Oaks, Ninshi London, Edward Thomson.

Book D, page 7.   John Allen Jr. to Isaac Low Jr. for 100 pds 157
A on Little Troublesome & Hogans Crs adj William Walker, Thomas
Conner, being part of grant to John Allen Sr.   Feb. 15, 1794.
John Browder, Andrew Martin.

Book D, page 8. John Allen & wife Elizabeth to Benjamin Moore for 50 pds 125 A on S side Pruets fork of Hogans Cr adj Thomas Preston, John Hodge, Thomas McCullough. Feb. 27, 1793. John Hallum, Joel Walker, John Matlock.

Book D, page 9. Samuel Bethell to John Johnston for 50 pds 120 A on Hogans Cr adj sd Johnston, Thomas Mullen. Mar. 9, 1793. Asa Dill, Richd. Stubblefield Jr., William McCollum.

Book D, page 10. James Appleton to John Coates Cox for 175 pds 200 A on head brs of Hogans Cr adj sd Appleton, Peter Oneil. Feb. 24, 1794. William Hornbuckle, John Appleton.

Book D, page 11. Edward Daniel of Henry Co., Va. to Richard Oakley for 100 pds 600 A on Matrimony Cr adj Samuel Gates, Virginia line, John Roach, Henry Grogan. Aug. 29, 1789. Joseph Hopper, Jenna Hoppe.

Book D, page 12. Andrew Wilson & wife Margaret to Thomas Horbuckle of Caswell Co. for 20 pds 35 A on Haw R adj sd Wilson, Jane Dilworth, Joseph Payn. June 5, 1793. William Hornbuckle, Henry Harding, Thomas Harding.

Book D, page 13. Peter Lewis to Thomas James for 153 pds 6 sh 8 p 150 A on Lickfork of Hogans Cr adj William Bethell, being part of grant from State to sd Lewis. June 21, 1792. John Thrasher, Elijah Brown, Lidda Toteson.

Book D, page 14. William Wright makes Gift Deed to sons James Wright and Nathan Wright for 20 sh paid by Martin Wright 157 A on a cr adj Martin Wright, James Patrick, John Wauford, Henry Brannock. Aug. 30, 1793. A. Philips, John Stockird.

Book D, page 15. Division of land of James Wright, deceased and leaving no will, between sons William Wright, Newton Wright and Martin Wright. Aug. 15, 1793. A. Philips. Ack in Open Court.

Book D, page 17. John Johnson, planter & son Joel Johnson to John Coates Cox, Doctor of Medicine, for 100 pds 100 A on Haw R adj Nelson, Joel Johnson. Nov. 8, 1792. Jere Poston, Jo Brawner.

Book D, page 18. William Wright, Newton Wright, Martin Wright to James Patrick for 10 pds 4 A on both sides Kinady Cr including old Mill Scot (?). Aug. 29, 1793. A. Philips.

Book D, page 19. Richard Pratt to Charles Galloway for 100 pds 177 A on Sharps Cr on S side Mayo Mountain adj sd Galloway, on S side of road leading from the Moravian Town to Petersburgh, also adj Thomas Pratt, John Pratt. Nov. 15, 1792. John Menzies, Joshua Smith, James Hunter.

Book D, page 19. Alexander Joyce Esq, High Sheriff, to Charles More for 20 pds 199 A on Richlands Cr adj John Rhodes, John Holmes, being land seized and sold to highest bidder to satisfy debt of estate of James Mulloy dec'd. Jan. 1, 1794. Peter Watson, Tho. Pound.

Book D, page 20. Alexander Joyce Esq, Sheriff to John Lenox, Merchant, for 30 pds 42 A on N side Highrock Road adj sd Lenox, the tract being sold by order of William Bethell, Clerk of Court to satisfy debt against estate of Peter Oneal dec'd. July 27, 1793. J. Holloway, Jno. C. Cox.

Book D, page 22. Daniel Allen the younger to John Lenox, merchant for 90 pds 180 A on Hogans Cr, it being part of the tract I and my brother John Allen now live, adj James Williams, Oneal. Feb. 17, 1794. John Holloway.

Book D, page 23. Samuel Moore to John Bennet for 50 pds 50 A on S side Haw R part of tract sd Moore bought from James Crayton. Aug. 8, 1793. A. Philips, Henry Lanier, Wm. Mobley.

Book D, page 24. Henry Burch & wife Susanna to John Fendel Carr for 150 pds 300 A on S side Mayo River to Buffalo Cr adj William Parks, Reuben Jackson, William Moore, Brysons Old Wagon Road. Mar. 12, 1788. Zach. King, Benjamin South, Little Berry Mays, Reuben Jackson.

Book D, page 25. Charles Galloway to Alexander Sneed for 100 pds Va. money 300 A on both sides Lickfork of Buffalo Island Cr adj John Hill, being tract granted in 1783 to William Lanson Lewis. Jan. 1, 1794. R. Galloway, John Menzies, Joel Stokes.

Book D, page 26. Isaac Wright of Guilford Co. to William Thorpe for 100 pds 162½ A on S side Troublesome Cr adj Guilford Co. line which is also the claiments own line. Feb. 26, ____. Will. Bethell.

Book D, page 27. John Glenn Sr. to William Glenn for 50 pds 150 A on both sides Reed Cr of Dan R adj Peter Watson, James Walker. Oct. 25, 1793. Joshua Smith, John Whitworth, Isaac Glen.

Book D, page 28. John Silman of Franklin Co., Ga. to David Barnet for 200 pds 150 A on Little Rockhouse Cr of Dan R adj Joel Walker. Nov. 27, 1793. Luke Bernard, Zadock Barnard, John Settle.

Book D, page 29. John Jones to Thomas Guttery for 150 pds 250 A on lower Hogans Cr adj John Hallum. July 31, 1793. R. Galloway, William Norris, Rice Brim.

Book D, page 30. William Fields to Alexander Joyce for 30 pds 100 A on Sharps Cr adj Tho. Henderson, Vernon. Feb. 1, 1794. John Norris, Joe T. Joyce.

Book D, page 31. Hance Laremore to John Hamilton of Guilford Co. for 150 pds 640 A crossing 3 brs adj George Judge (but now Robert Goins' line), Lacy. May 30, 1794. Alex. Joyce, Hubbard Peeples.

Book D, page 32. John Harper to Abraham Hendrickson for 30 pds 166 A on Little Buffalo Cr. Feb. 26, 1793. Nathaniel Linder, Nathaniel Tatum, Robert Small.

Book D, page 33. Patrick Wardlow to John Haynes for 40 sh 43 A on headwaters of Little Troublesome Cr adj sd Haynes, Jesse Broughton. May 10, 1794. Sarah Haines, Daniel Haines.

Book D, page 34.   Martin Wisenor to Henry Wisenor for 50 pds 184
A on High Rock Cr of Haw R adj John Wheler, John Bourk, John W.
Jones.   May 27, 1794.   A. Philips, Benjn. Spencer.

Book D, page 35.   John Rowland to David Rowland for 100 pds 137
A on both sides Haw R adj Christapher Vandergraph, William Jones,
James Wright, this being tract laid out unto John Rowland as one
of the claiments to real estate of George Rowland dec'd.   Apr.
5, 1794.   John Hallum, George Hallum.

Book D, page 36.   John Coventon to Beverly Warwick for 50 pds
117 A on Wolf Island Cr adj Patrick Wardlow, Robert Martin,
Abraham Philips, John Hains.   Mar. 25, 1794.   James Hall, Henry
Govin (Gorin?).

Book D, page 37.   Robert Boak to John Boak for 100 pds 200 A
between the two Troublesome Crs adj Domanick Hilland, Widow
McCaleb, John Odineal, Simon Dunn.   May 30, 1794.   Thomas Scott,
William Boak.

Book D, page 38.   Thomas Thomson of Davidson Co. to John Moore
for 80 pds 400 A on N side Troublesome Cr adj William Scott,
Francis McBride, Iron Works.   Nov. 14, 1788.   Samuel Thomson,
Robert Thompson.

Book D, page 39.   State of N.C. to Alexander Martin for bravery
and zeal as officer in Continental Line 2000 A in Middle District
Territory Southwest of Ohio R, S side Duck R on both sides Tom-
bigby Cr & including Pruets Lick adj Robert Goodlow, General
Green, James Pearsal.   Dec. 17, 17__.   (Issued by J. Glasgow,
Secretary to Gov. Alexander Martin.)

Book D, page 40.   State of N.C. to John Odineal, Assignee for
Archibald Yarbrough, 480 A on W side Wolf Island Cr adj Edward
Perkins.   Nov. 17, 1790.

Book D, page 41.   William Douglass of Rowan Co. to Robert Kimbrough of Caswell Co. for 116 pds Va. money 240 A on Wolf Island
Cr adj Caswell Co. line.   Feb. 11, 1793.   Saml. Watt, Peter Marten.

Book D, page 42.   Jacob McCollum to Isaac McCollum for 50 pds his
equal foruth of tract on N side Hogans Cr, ref being made to deed
of John McCollum to Isaac McCollum & others.   Apr. 14, 1794.
William Bethell, Nimshi London.

Book D, page 43.   Thomas Caldwell Brent & wife Mary to Alexander
Joyce for 30 pds 145 A on both sides Hickory Cr of Mayo R adj
Thomas Crawley, Stokes Co. line, John Ruson.   Mar. 1, 1794.
Adam Tate.

Book D, page 44.   Nathaniel Linder to James Wright for 30 pds
63 A including land whereon Widow Hubbard did live, on E fork
of Jacobs Cr adj Richard Hingson.   May 28, 1794.   Saml. Watt,
Thomas Lomax.

Book D, page 45.   John Stockard to John Howell for 146 pds 42 A
on both sides Rocky fork of Jacobs Cr above the Mill Dam adj
Low.   1794.   James Hays, Nathl. Linder, Betsey Howell.

Book D, page 46.   Chesley Barnes to Zachariah King for 50 pds 50
A on S side Mayo R.   Dec. 17, 1792.   James Jackson, William King,
Tho. Jackson.

Book D, page 47. Joseph Cloud Thrasher to Reverend Thomas Mullen for 5 sh 1 A during his natural life and after his death to be for use of public for building a house of Worship. June 6, 1793. William McCollum, William Cockrill, Richd. Stubblefield, William Bethell.

Book D, page 48. Robert Warren to William Fields for 80 pds Va. money 100 A on Sharps Cr adj Thomas Henderson, Vernon. Apr. 8, 1792. Sam. Henderson, Joshua Smith.

Book D, page 49. Edward Daniel of Henry Co., Va. to James Clay-brook for 100 pds 100 A on Stewards Cr adj Farlour, Va. line. Feb. 6, 1793. John Grogan, William Grogan, John Clifton.

Book D, page 50. Thomas Skinner & wife Sarah to Leaven Downs 100 Spanish Milled Dollars 60 A on S side Wolf Island Cr, being tract purchased from Christapher Dudley. Nov. 23, 1793. Wm. McCollum, John Thrasher, Wm. Traynum.

Book D, page 51. John London to Leaven Downs for 10 pds 100 A on Wolf Island Cr adj John McCubbin. Dec. 3, 1793. Nimshi London, Edward Thompson.

Book D, page 52. John Simmons to William Standard of Caswell for 25 pds 100 A on Burches Cr, fuller inf in records of Guilford Co. Aug. 28, 1792. Henry Henricks, Peter Watson.

Book D, page 53. Mary Stratton to Stephen Sanders for 50 pds 145 A on Gr Rockhouse Cr adj William Jones, Abraham Philips, James Saunders, being land granted by State to Minor March. July 16, 1792. Cornelius Wright, William Hubbard.

Book D, page 54. James Reagan to William Southerland for 50 pds 200 A on Blews Cr adj Christapher Zeaglor. May 16, 1794. William Bethell.

Book D, page 55. John London to Jehu London for 10 sh 207½ A on S side Stones fork of Wolf Island Cr and on brs of Quaqua Cr adj Zachariah Bryant. Dec. 2, 1793. Edward Thompson, John McCubbin, Henry Wall.

Book D, page 56. State of N.C. to Thomas Faulconer 125 A on S fork of Piney Cr adj own line, Robert Small, David Moore, Robert Boak. Dec. 20, 1791.

Book D, page 57. John London to Nimshi London for 10 sh 207½ A on both sides Stones fork of Wolf Island Cr adj Patterson, Bryant. Dec. 2, 1793. Edward Thompson, John McCubbin, Henry Wall.

Book D, page 58. John Reynolds of Lincoln Co. to William Magniss of aforesaid Co. for 60 pds 250 A on Bufflow Cr of Broad R, being part of grant by State to Thomas Reynolds Dec. 19, 1753 & then conveyed to his son John Reynolds. Apr. 4, 1792. David Ramsey, John Reynolds.

Book D, page 59. Ann Tate, Exrx of Woody Tate dec'd of Caswell Co. to Peter Oneal Esq for 13,000 lbs of Good Tobacco 35 7/8 A in Caswell Co. on Countryline Cr adj Hays, Rice. May 19, 1791. John Reid, John Herbin Jr.

Book D, page 60. Alexander Joyce, Sheriff, to Thomas Brent for 6 pds 145 A, land seized for settlement of debt against James Mulloy Adm to be paid to Charles Bruce, Com. Confiscated Property. Feb. 10, 1794.

Book D, page 61. Alexander Joyce, High Sheriff to Robert Cummins for 5 pds 10 sh 193 A on Troublesome Cr, being land seized by order of Court & sold to highest bidder to satisfy debt of James Mulloy dec'd. May 27, 1794. Alex. Brown, Lewis Cockrill.

Book D, page 62. William Boyd to Thomas Thompson of Guilford Co. for 100 pds 334 A on both sides Little Troublesome Cr & crossing one br of Hogans Cr adj John Hallum Esq, Widow Diamond. June 6, 1794. Henry Brannock, Sam Curry.

Book D, page 63. William Hubbard & wife Esther to Gordon Smith for 187 pds 10 sh 300 A on Hogans Cr adj Moravian line, Hugh Reed. Apr. 24, 1794. Henry Brannock, Wm. Wright.

Book D, page 64. William Bethell to Alexander McClaren for 50 pds 200 A on Rockhouse Cr adj Minor March, James Saunders, sd McClaren. Aug. 26, 1794. A. Philips.

Book D, page 65. John Boyd to Samuel Watt for 250 pds 400 A in Caswell Co. on both sides Hogans Cr. Oct. 10, 1793. Ezekiel Jones, William Bethell, R. Williams.

Book D, page 66. Joseph Erwin of Guilford Co. to John Lemond for 30 pds 500 A on Sulpher fork of Red River in Tenese Co. adj Collo. Ezekiel Polk, being land granted by State to Peggy Allen Sept. 15, 1787, sold to Turner Williams and then to sd Erwin. June 1, 1793. George Lemon, Joseph Lemond.

Book D, page 67. William Gillaspy, Exr of Est of Patrick Campbell dec'd of Cumberland Co. to Leaven Mitchel for 100 pds 300 A in Sumner Co. on Cumberland R. Apr. 25, 1794. Nathl. Linder, Mary Linder.

Book D, page 68. Leavin Mitchell to Elisha Bernard 150 pds 230 A on both sides Town Cr. Mar. 20, 1794. Edward Williams, Peter Atchison.

Book D, page 69. Samuel Brown to Robert Brown for 50 pds 103 A on Troublesome Cr called No. 3, being his share of two tracts his father, James Brown dec'd, possessed. Land divided by Thomas Lomax, Thomas Lowe, Benjamin McFarlin, Nathl. Linder, Commissioners. Sept. 17, 1793. A. Philips, Sutton McColister.

Book D, page 72. Philip Gates to Alexander Martin Esq for 50 pds 98 A on S side Dan R crossing Cokers Cr adj sd Martin, being land first granted to Benjamin Gates and then by deed to Philip Gates. June 17, 1792. R. Martin, Tho. Rogers.

Book D, page 73. Hugh Brown to Samuel Brown for 50 pds 103 A on Jacobs Cr adj John Cunningham Jr., Sutton McColister, called No. 6, being his share of two tracts owned by his father, James Brown dec'd, and divided by Commissioners Thomas Lomax, Thomas Lowe, Benjamin McFarlin, Nathaniel Linder. Sept. 17, 1793. A. Philips.

Book D, page 74. John Harper to Jesse Hinton for 50 pds 150 A on Little Buffalow Cr adj Abraham Hendricks. June 21, 1794. Joseph Hopper, Joseph Odell, Lewis Hopper.

Book D, page 75.   John Winchester to John Winchester Jr. for 50 pds 150 A on N side Haw R.   Aug. 9, 1794.   A. Philips, Samuel McSparan, Robt. Larrimore.

Book C, page 76.   John Martin & wife Catreen to William Cummins for 50 pds 200 A on Jumping Br adj Linder, Browder.   July 12, 1794.   Tho. Pound, Lawrence Porter.

Book C, page 77.   Lawrance Bankson & wife Sarah to Aron Cantrill for 100 pds land on both sides Wolf Island Cr adj sd Bankson. Nov. 4, 1792.   Jacob Cantrill, John Martin.

Book D, page 78.   Lawrence Bankson & wife Sarah to Aron Cantrill for 40 pds 34 A on N fork of Wolf Island Cr adj Talitha Browder, John Linder.   Dec. 4, 1794.   Jacob Cantrill, John Martin.

Book D, page 79.   Edward Taylor of Roan Co. to Baily Martin for 80 pds 150 A on Hogans Cr.   July 24, 1793.   Danl. Atkins, John Cantrill, Wm. Philips.

Book D, page 80.   Daniel Atkins, Atty for William Beran Godhead of S.C., to Heirs of James Martin dec'd of Montgomery Co. for 50 pds 146 A on Hogans Cr adj Zebidee Savage.   Aug. 27, 1794.

Book D, page 81.   Thomas Chance to Samuel Watt for 42 pds 43 A on Pruets fork of Hogans Cr adj sd Watt.   Aug. 23, 1794.   Robert Harris, William Hedrick, John Hedrick.

Book D, page 82.   Robert Harris, Atty for John Harris, to Samuel Watt for 100 pds 120 A on both sides Pruets fork of Hogans Cr adj sd Watt, Abraham Philips, being grant by Granville to Thompson Harris dec'd.   Feb. 10, 1794.   N. Williams Jr., John Watt.

Book D, page 83.   Theodorick Stubblefield & wife Fanny to William Bethell for 50 pds 45 A on Pruets fork of Hogans Cr adj sd Stubblefield, being part of grant by Granville to Thompson Harris dec'd and willed to his son Thompson.   Mar. 10, 1789.   Richard Stubblefield, John Thrasher, Thomas Chambers.

Book D, page 84.   William Allen of Warren Co. to William Bethell for 50 pds 100 A on Hogans Cr adj William Weybin, Zachariah Thacker, Richard Ellis, Joseph McClain, James Horseford, being a grant in 1784 to sd Allen.   July 25, 1789. Samuel Bethell, Henry Tourant.

Book D, page 85.   William Baker to William Bethell for 50 pds 37 A on Hogans Cr adj Charles Dean.   May 11, 1791.   Samuel Bethell, George Burnett.

Book D, page 86.   James Horsford to William Bethell for 20 pds 25 A on Hogans Cr adj sd Horsford on Chambers Mill Road, Joseph McClain.   Aug. 25, 1788.   Jno Horsford, Henry Tourant, Robt.Harris.

Book D, page 87.   Robert Harris to William Bethell for 80 pds 120 A on Pruets fork of Hogans Cr adj John Horsford, Samuel Watt, including plantation whereon lived Thompson Harris dec'd.   Dec. 10, 1793.   Richard Bethell, Suckey Bethell, Jency Bethell.

Book D, page 88.   Alexander Joyce Esq, High Sheriff, to William Bethell for 16 pds 360 A adj Wm. Trainum, sd land seized & sold to highest bidder for debt of est of John Odineal dec'd recovered by Martha Fletcher for Sherwood Toney and wife, also Isaac

Thrasher. Aug. 22, 1794. Suckey Bethell.

Book D, page 89. Job Loftis to Richard Marr for 50 pds 100 A on
Lickfork of Hogans Cr adj Henry Dixon, Charles Gilley, John Mount.
May 7, 1789. Daniel Atkins, Joseph Owen, James Owen.

Book D, page 90. James Powell to Richard Marr for 50 pds 34 A
on Lickfork of Hogans Cr adj John Mount. Oct. 20, 1790. Zach.
Sneed, Thomas Carter, John M. Marr.

Book D, page 91. Richard Marr to William Russell for 20 pds 8 A
on Wolf Island Cr adj John Smith, being land bought of Hugh
Challes. Aug. 26, 1793. Thomas Oakes, Lawrence Porter, Hugh
Mills.

Book D, page 92. Robert Martin to Bailey Martin for 50 pds 106½
A on Wolf Island Cr adj Samuel Herrin, Abraham Philips. Nov. 16,
1793. William Martin, James Philips.

Book D, page 93. Walter Hill to Edward Richardson for 20 pds 83
A on S side Haw R adj William Robertson, Moses Campbell. Aug. 5,
1793. John Richardson, Walter Hill.

Book D, page 94. Alexander Brown to Levi King for 20 pds 40 A
adj sd King, Thomas Massey, Alexander Martin Esq. Aug. 26, 1794.
Nathaniel Linder, William Johnson.

Book D, page 95. James Saunders to John King for 10 pds 60 A on
Rockhouse and Piney Crs adj Robert Small, Benjamin Haggard,
Mathies Mount. Nov. 26, 1794. A. Philips, Elizabeth Tatum,
Elizabeth Sanders.

Book D, page 96. William Kellum to John Dale for 50 pds 220 A
on Green Springs of Mayo R adj Galloway. 1794. William Motley,
Theophilus Watkins.

Book D, page 97. David Hanby and Humphry Brooks to Theophilus
Watkins for 9,000 lbs tobacco 120 A on S side Mayo R. Sept. 26,
1793. John Harbour, George Hunter.

Book D, page 98. John Hill and William Hill, Heirs of Rev.
William Hill dec'd, to James Scales for 200 pds 300 A on S side
Dan R. Oct. 1, 1794. Elizabeth Whitworth, Elizabeth Larrimore,
M. Hardin.

Book D, page 99. Alexander Lyall & wife Elizabeth to William
Motley for 50 pds 100 A on N side Mayo R adj Richard Cardwell.
Mar. 14, 1793. Umphry Brooks, James Kelly, George Hunter, James
Asbury.

Book D, page 100. State of N.C. to Henry Scales 50 A on Buffelow Island Cr adj own land. June 27, 1793.

Book D, page 101. State of N.C. to Joshua Hopper 500 A on Island Cr called Tacketts Br of Smith R and crossing two brs of
Matrimony Cr. July 9, 1794.

Book D, page 102. Nathaniel Williams to Joseph Garner 10 pds 45
A on both sides Cabbin Br of Hogans Cr. Aug. 22, 1792. A.
Philips.

Book D, page 103. John Coats Cox, Doctor of Medicine, to Ann Nelson of Guilford Co. for 100 pds 100 A on Haw R and High Rock Road adj Joel Johnson, being part of grant to John Johnson. Sept. 8, 1794. John Smith, William Nelson, Deborah Cox.

Book D, page 104. Alexander Joyce Esq, High Sheriff, to Walter Martin for 9 pds 19 A adj No. 4 in division of estate of Soloman West dec'd, being land seized by order of court for debt of est of Soloman West dec'd. Sept. 14, 1794. William Bethell.

Book D, page 105. John Pritchet to John Lewis for 20 pds 26 A crossing one br of Saxapahaw R adj sd Lewis, George Dilworth, Francis Hodge. Mar. 29, 1794. William Connoly, George Dilworth.

Book D, page 106. John Lain & wife Rachel to Priscilla Gibson for 83.6.8 100 A on Lickfork of Hogans Cr adj Thomas Williams, being grant to Thadeus Owen, thence to James Tomlinson, thence to Jno. Tomlinson and then to sd Lane. Sept. 7, 1793. Dennis Kelley, Wm. Bradberry.

Book D, page 107. Charles Moore to Soloman Webster for 150 pds 200 A on both sides Conners Br of Troublesome Cr adj sd Webster, Robert Barr, Mathew George. Nov. 22, 1794. Walter Martin, William Conner.

Book D, page 108. David Vaughan to Charles Shickle for 50 pds 25½ A adj Thomas Settle. Nov. 14, 1791. Thomas Settle.

Book D, page 109. Edward Williams to James Daniel for 200 Spanish Mill'd dollars 150 A on Wolf Island Cr adj James Cantrill, Isaac Cantrill. May 1, 1794. James Williams, John Granger.

Book D, page 110. John Haines to Daniel Haines for 20 pds 50 A on Little Troublesome Cr adj Hugh Harkins. May 7, 1794. Cynthia Philips, A. Philips.

Book D, page 111. Nancy Mulloy to William Case for 50 pds 136 A made to her by Alexander Joyce Esq High Sheriff on Nov. 26, 1793. Nov. 27, 1793. Robert Cumming, George Lemond.

Book D, page 112. Mathew Amberson to William Conner for 79 pds 150 A on S side Little Troublesome Cr adj Andrew Scott, being tract whereon Amberson now lives. Nov. 24, 1794. Robert Barr, William Amberson.

Book D, page 113. William Bethell, Atty for Benjamin Cook of Pittsylvania Co., Va. to Robert Boak for 50 pds 200 A on Little Troublesome Cr adj sd Boak, McCalab. Aug. 29, 1794. Alex. Joyce, John Bradley, Jo. T. Joyce.

Book D, page 114. Division of land by James Hodge and brothers: No. 1 William Hodge 253 A on Hogans Cr adj Thomas McCullock. No. 2 James Hodge 253 A. No. 3 John Charles Hodge 253 A on Hogans Cr. Survey by A. Philips. Sept. 7,1790. John Allen, John Wilson, David Settle, James McCarrell.

Book D, page 116. Division of Est of James Brown dec'd by Commissioners Thomas Massey, Thomas Lowe, Thomas Lomax, Benjamin McFarlin and Nathaniel Linder. No. 1 David Brown 103 A on Big Troublesome Cr adj Richard Henderson. No. 2 William Brown 103 A.

No. 3 Samuel Brown 103 A crossing br of Rockhouse Cr adj Richard
Henderson. No. 4 Robert Brown 103 A. No. 5 Elijah Brown 103 A.
No. 6 Hugh Brown 103 A. No. 7 James Brown, Assignee to John
Brown, 107 A. Margaret Brown, widow of James Brown dec'd Right
of Dower on No. 5. Oct. 10, 1792. Surveyed by A. Philips.

Book D, page 119. Division of Est of George Rowland dec'd by
John Stanford, Alexander Walker, Michael Caffey, Walter Hill,
Robert Small: No. 1 John Rowland 137 A on both sides Haw R adj
James Wright, Christopher Vandergriff, William Jones, John Sprout.
No. 2 David Rowland 137 A. No. 3 Benjamin Rowland 137 A. No.
4 James Rowland 137 A. No. 5 George Rowland 137 A. Sept. 22,
1792. Surveyed by A. Philips.

Book D, page 121. State of N.C. to John Oliver 50 A on Hogans
Cr adj own land, Robert Gilleland. June 27, 1793.

Book D, page 122. State of N.C. to Job Baker 100 A on Brushy
fork of Rockhouse Cr adj Joseph Cunningham, James Brown. July
11, 1788.

Book D, page 123. State of N.C. to James Joice 55 A on Cabbin
Br of Mayo R adj own land, Deatherage. June 27, 1793.

Book D, page 124. State of N.C. to Robert Nelson 200 A on both
sides Pounding Mill Br of Jacobs Cr adj own land, Robert Martin,
James Hays, Samuel Martin. Dec. 20, 1791.

Book D, page 125. State of N.C. to Samuel Nelson 200 A on both
sides Long Br of Jacobs Cr adj Francis Young, Samuel Martin.
Dec. 20, 1791.

Book D, page 126. David Peeples of Green Co., Ga. to Lewis Peeples for 100 pds 31 A on Greens Br of Jacobs Cr adj William Green.
Nov. 19, 1794.

Book D, page 127. Elizabeth Peeples of Green Co., Ga. wife of
David Peeples relinquishes Right of Dower for tract to be sold
to Lewis Peeples. Nov. 19, 1794. James Jenkins, Hubbard Peeples,
Burwell Peeples.

Book D, page 127. State of N.C. to William Clark Jr. 16 A on
Pruets fork of Hogans Cr adj Widow Allen, Samuel Watt. July 9,
1794.

Book D, page 128. State of N.C. to William Clark Jr. 40 A on
Hogans Cr adj own land. July 9, 1794.

Book D, page 129. Thomas Key & wife Mary to Samuel Watt for 40
pds 40 A adj sd Watt. Dec. 25, 1793. James Watt, Bartlet Mathis.

Book D, page 130. Thomas Adams to Samuel Watt for 400 pds 176 A
on Hogans Cr adj sd Watt, James Hays. Feb. 25, 1795. John Matlock, John Odineal, Alex. Joyce.

Book D, page 131. William Wilson of Pendleton Co., S.C. to
James Taylor for 50 pds 115 A on High Rock Cr of Haw R adj sd
Wilson. Jan. 24, 1795. William Harbin, William Hornbuckle,
Martin Wisiner.

Book D, page 132. Robert Boak to Moses Yell for 26.18.1½ 35 A

on Big Troublesome Cr adj sd Yell, John Waaford, William Jones.
1795. John Stanford, George Rowland.

Book D, page 133. John Leak Esq to Thomas Searcy of Guilford Co.
for $10 ½ A on NW side Dan R adj Lott No. 19, Henry Street. Feb.
26, 1795. A. Philips.

Book D, page 134. John Simmons to James McCubbin for 20 pds 43
3/4 A on both sides Burchfields fork of Wolf Island Cr adj Peter
Martin, William Patterson, Francis Patterson. Dec. 10, 1794.
A. Philips, Nicholas McCubbin, William Patterson.

Book D, page 135. John McKinny to James Roach for 55 pds 200 A
on both sides Little Rockhouse Cr. Jan. 26, 1795. A. Philips,
Joseph Street.

Book D, page 136. Thomas Hatfield to Thomas Fulford for 10 pds
36 A on Lickfork Cr. Oct. 12, 1793. William McCollum, Martha
McCollum, Cloud McCollum.

Book D, page 137. Sarah Clegg to John McCune (also written
Mecune) for 50 pds 50 A adj Joshua Smith, Jarratt Patterson,
Andrew Joyce. Apr. 11, 1791. Nehemiah Vernon, Charles Gordon,
David Dalton, John Whitworth.

Book D, page 138. Benjamin Spencer to Robert Hatrick for 250
pds 194 A on N side Haw R on High Rock Cr adj William & John
Herbin. Feb. 12, 1795. A. Philips, Saml. Corry.

Book D, page 139. Thomas North to William Russell for 50 pds
50 A on Woolesland Cr adj Richard Marr, Dicks Road, William Bethell. 1794. Samuel Smith, John Smith.

Book D, page 140. Nathaniel Linder to Henry King for 150 pds
174½ A on Big Troublesome Cr adj William Short, Mitchel, Thomas,
Massey, Thomas Henderson. May 27, 1794. A. Philips, John Lowe.

Book D, page 141. John Winchester to Coleman Winchester for 50
pds 118 A on N side Haw R adj James Martin, Stephen Mitchel.
Aug. 9, 1794. A. Philips, Samuel McSparan, Robert Larimore.

Book D, page 142. James Lord to John Jones for 50 pds 94 A on
Wolf Island Cr adj David Morris, William Harrison, Thomas Pound,
William Young. Aug. 29, 1794. Tho. Pound, Bn. Williams, Jse.
McCarrell.

Book D, page 144. (p. 143 omitted) John Haines to John Linder
for 150 pds 300 A on Little Troublesome Cr adj John Thomson, Hugh
Harkins former line but now Solomon Webster. Dec. 20, 1794. A.
Philips, Vincent Whealer.

Book D, page 145. John Haines to John Linder for 100 pds 150 A
on both sides Little Troublesome Cr adj Elijah Haines, Jonathon
Haines, Daniel Haines, being land bought of Adam Holker. Dec.
20, 1794. Vincent Whealer, A. Philips.

Book D, page 146. David Lovell to Robert Hutson for 50 pds 231
A on S side Piney fork of Town Cr adj sd Lovell. Feb. 27, 1794.
A. Philips, H. Larrimore, Drury Williams.

Book D, page 147. William Johnson to Gideon Johnson Jr. for 100 pds 272 A on both sides Moses Cr adj Allen Walker, William Astin, Gideon Johnson, William Howard. Feb. 13, 1795. A. Philips, William Bethell, Danl. Atkins.

Book D, page 148. John McCarrell to Bartlett Estes for 75 pds 110 A on Piney Fork of Troublesome Cr. Aug. 26, 1794. A. Philips, Tho. Pound, Thos. Lowe.

Book D, page 149. Christopher Ziglar & wife Elizabeth of Stokes Co. to Joseph Ladd for 160 pds 160 A in counties of Stokes and Rockingham on forks of Bilus Cr adj sd Ladd, William Souther- land. Jan. 10, 1795. Anthony Bitting, William Southerland.

Book D, page 150. Isaac Clark Esq, High Sheriff to William Bet- hell for 26 pds 11 sh 200 A adj John Horsford (formerly Zach Thacker), Samuel Wall (formerly Robert Harris), John Allison, this land being seized by order of Guilford Co. Court to satisfy debt of Nathan Thacker. Mar. 15, 1794. A. Philips, Saml. Watt.

Book D, page 151. Naman Roberts and Ezra Roberts to Sneed Strong for 90 pds 3 A on N side Dan R adj sd Strong, John Lemon Sr., Est of James Roberts dec'd. Feb. 23, 1795. John Strong, James Rose.

Book D, page 152. Christopher Ziglar & wife Elizabeth of Stokes Co. to William Southerland for 160 pds 160 A in counties of Stokes and Rockingham on forks of Belews Cr adj sd Southerland. Jan. 10, 1795. Joseph Ladd, Anthony Bitting.

Book D, page 153. Sarah Clegg to Thomas Lewellin for 100 pds Va. money 150 A adj Watson Gentry, William Jennings, James Siers. Apr. 24, 1792. Samuel Gann, Thomas Lewellin.

Book D, page 154. John Jones to Amey Overbey for 100 pds 123 A on Little Rockhouse Cr. Feb. 26, 1795. A. Philips, John Brown.

Book D, page 155. State of N.C. to Moses Garrison 18 A on Lick- fork of Hogans Cr adj sd Garrison, David Settle. Nov. 20,1791.

Book D, page 156. Shadrack Yeoman, Stokes Yeoman, Lègatees and surviving exrs of est of Drury Yeoman Sr. dec'd to Samuel Call- and, Gent, merchant of Pittsylvania Co., Va. for 650 pds Va. money 300 A on N side Dan R on Eagle Falls adj George Peay Sr., John May. Mar. 26, 1795. John May, Sus Yeoman, Sarah Lewis, Betsy Davis, Jno. Menzies, Robert Galloway, Jno Bellanfont.

Book D, page 157. Alexander Joyce Esq, High Sheriff to Robert Galloway & Company for 60.11.5 187 A on N side Dan R adj Joseph Scales, land seized by order of court to satisfy debt of Batte C. Lacey. May 29, 1795. Nathl Linder, Peter Watson.

Book D, page 158. George W. Overton certifies that he relin- quished his highest bid on above land to Robert Galloway & Co. Feb. 27, 1794. John Menzies.

Book D, page 158. State of N.C. to Mathew Peggs 50 A on N side Mayo R adj sd Peggs, William Mills. July 9, 1794.

Book D, page 159. James Martin to Coalman Winchester for 5 pds 9 3/4 A on N side Haw R adj sd Martin. May 26, 1795. A. Philips, John May.

Book D, page 160. John Oliver to Peter Oliver for 20 pds 50 A on Upper Hogans Cr adj Robert Gilleland. May 26, 1795.

Book D, page 161. Robert McKenny of Guilford Co. to William Dillon of Guilford Co. for 60 pds 150 A on both sides Reeds Cr of Balues Cr adj Surry Co. 1795. Nathan Dillon, Z. D. Brasher.

Book D, page 162. Nehemiah Vernon to Thomas Joyce for 10 pds Proclamation Money 30 A on Upper Double Cr & Mayo R adj John and Isaac Vernon. Feb. 14, 1795. Robert Joyce, John Vernon, Isaac Vernon.

Book D, page 163. Thomas Henderson to John Lowe for 200 pds 262½ A on both sides Troublesome Cr adj Baker, Cunningham. Mar. 5, 1795.

Book D, page 164. Frances Young of Abievil, S.C. to Thomas Lowe for 133 pds 300 A on Jacobs Cr adj sd Lowe. Dec. 14, 1790. Robt. Galloway, James Hayes Sr.

Book D, page 165. Nathaniel Linder to John Lowe for 130 pds 36½ A on B Troublesome Cr adj sd Lowe, being land bought of Thomas Green. May 27, 1794. A. Philips, Henry King.

Book D, page 166. Henry Harden of Wilks Co., Ga. to John Mathews for 250 pds 150 A adj Andrew Joyce, Elijah Joyce, Sarah Gentry, Benjamin Cook. Aug. 16, 1793. Joshua Smith, Jarrat Patterson.

Book D, page 167. Solomon Webster to Charles Moore for 155 pds 200 A on both sides Conners Br of Troublesome Cr adj Robert Barr, Matthew George, Hugh Harkins. Jan. 7, 1795. Thomas Thompson, Rebecca Henry.

Book D, page 168. Division of Land of Henry Work dec'd to orphans by Commissioners Hubbard Peeples, Hugh Lynch, James Patrick, Burrel Peeples, William Lemond. No. 1 Joseph T. Joyce in right of his wife 249 A on N side Haw R. No. 2 Robert Maxwell in right of his wife 209 A on N bank of Haw R. No. 3 Margaret and Jane Work 304 A on Marrs Fork of Haw R. Mar. 4, 1795.

Book D, page 169. Margaret Work, late widow of Henry Work, relinquishes her Right of Dower to No. 1 and No. 2 and will share No. 3. A. Philips.

Book D, page 170. John Stanford to John Bennett for $112.00 56 A on S side Haw R adj sd Bennett, Edward Richardson. Dec. 4, 1794. A. Philips, Nancy Stanford, Elizabeth Stanford.

Book D, page 171. Abner Shenault to Alexander Russell for 100 pds 200 A on both sides upper Hogans Cr adj Zaza Brasher, Charles Bruce. Feb. 26, 1795. A. Philips, Isaac Wright.

Book D, page 172. John Horsford & wife Elizabeth to John Watt for 100 pds 200 A on Pruetts fork of Hogans Cr adj Hannah Harris, Nathan Thacker, William Obanion, Dixie Ferry Road. Feb. 14, 1794. Saml. Watt, Ezekiel Jones.

Book D, page 173. State of N.C. to Josiah Settle 100 A on Pruetts fork of Hogans Cr adj John Matlock, Peter Oneal. May 16, 1787.

Book D, page 174. Cornelus Davis of Caswell Co. to Joseph Garner for 50 pds 103 A on Hogans Cr, being part of old Savage tract. Mar. 3, 1795. John Watt, Thomas Davis.

Book D, page 175. Isaac Philips to John Spurrier for 28 pds 150 A on both sides Big Rockhouse Cr adj Theophilus Spurrier, Alexander McClaran, John Mount (formerly Thomas Loyd's). Oct. 1, 1794. A. Philips, Alex. McClaran.

Book D, page 176. William Coventon of Washington Co., Ga. to John Grant of Caswell Co. for 100 pds 500 A on Whetstone Cr of Dan R adj George Peay, John Thomas. Nov. 17, 1792. Isaac McClaran, David Walker.

Book D, page 177. Abner Parrot to William Ward for 40 pds 99 A & 60 rods on Duncans Br adj John Challes. May 23, 1795. Drury Smith, Samuel Bower Hawkins.

Book D, page 178. Josiah Settle to Benjamin Settle for 4 sh 100 A adj sd Settle, Peter Oneal, John Matlock. Oct. 22, 1793. David Settle, John Wardlow, James Baitman.

Book D, page 179. State of N.C. to Joseph McColock 73 A on Hogans Cr adj own land, Hodge. July 9, 1794.

Book D, page 180. State of N.C. to Luke Barnard 200 A on Gr Rockhouse Cr adj own land, John Watt. July 9, 1794.

Book D, page 181. State of N.C. to William Harrison 50 A on Wolf Island Cr adj own land, Patrick Wardlow, Guy Vermilion. June 27, 1793.

Book D, page 182. State of N.C. to John McCarill 200 A on Gr Rockhouse Cr adj John Perkle, Robert Walker. July 11, 1788.

Book D, page 183. State of N.C. to Jacob Cantrill 170 A on N fork Wolf Island Cr adj Henry Hendrickson, Luke Bernett. July 11, 1788.

Book D, page 184. Benjamin Spencer to William Herbin & John Herbin for 144 pds 144 A on Haw R adj Robert Hatrick. Feb. 10, 1795. A. Philips, J. Charter.

Book D, page 185. Elizabeth Oneal to Lancelott Johnston of Caswell Co. for 150 pds 150 A on Hogans Cr & Country line Cr adj John Lenox. Feb. 16, 1795. Hugh Corigan, Thomas Johnston, Robert A. Brown.

Book D, page 186. Lancelott Johnston of Caswell Co. to John Lenox for 150 pds 150 A on Hogans Cr & Countryline adj sd Lenox, High Rock Road, Hugh Gwyn. Arp. 25, 1795. John Brown, J. Charters.

Book D, page 187. William Wilson to John Burk for 100 pds 268 A on High Rock Cr of Haw R. Jan. 27, 1792. William Herbin, John Herbin, Jere. Poston.

Book D, page 188. John Fields, Deputy Sheriff to Robert Boke 1 negro man Reubin, property of Joseph Street. Aug. 27, 1795. John Whitworth, Richd. Bethell.

Book D, page 188. Peter Wall to Benjamin Forsyth of Stokes Co. for 100 pds 100 A on Big Rockhouse Cr within 1 mile of the Courthouse adj Robert Galloway, Luke Bernard, John Wall. May 29, 1795. Drury Williams, John Arnold.

Book D, page 189. Abner Parrot to John Milbry of Pitsilvania Co., Va. for 40 pds 99 A & 60 perch on Duncans Br adj John Challes. May 23, 1795. Drury Smith, Samuel Bower Hawkins.

Book D, page 190. Alexander Joyce Esq, High Sheriff to Elizabeth Oneal for 3 pds land adj John Lenox, Hugh Gwyn, being land sold to highest bidder for debt of Est of Peter Oneal dec'd. Feb. 14, 1794. John Hunter, John Bradley.

Book D, page 191. Josiah Settle to Benjamin Settle for 5 sh 28 A. Jan. 2, 1792. David Settle, Jemima Settle.

Book D, page 192. Thrasher McCallum to Isaac McCallum of Wake Co. for 50 pds 300 A allotted to me by my father Daniel McCallum. Aug. 24, 1795. William Bethell, Cloud Thrasher.

Book D, page 193. Robert Kimbrough of Caswell Co. to James Grant Jr. of Caswell Co. for 200 pds 240 A on Wolf Island Cr adj Caswell line. Aug. 25, 1795. William Bethell, James Appleton.

Book D, page 194. James Claybrook to John Grogan of Henry Co., Va. for 100 pds Va. money 100 A adj Virginia line, Farlow. Aug. 29, 1795. John Menzies, Jno. Peay.

Book D, page 195. John Baker to Charles Baker for 300 pds 128 A on Big Troublesome Cr adj Thomas Massey, Samuel Brown. Aug. 11, 1795. Nathl. Linder, William Jones, Aaron Allen.

Book D, page 196. Simpson Harris to Robert Wray & Andrew Wray for $1,500.00 560 A on Little Troublesome Cr & brs of Pruets fork of Hogans Cr. Aug. 27, 1795. Alex. Joyce, Duke Williams, William Conner.

Book D, page 197. Laurance Bankson to Robert Walker for 40 pds 121 A on Little Rockhouse Cr adj David Lovell, Charles Galloway, William Elliot, Andrew Roberson, John Abbit. Feb. 25, 1792. John Linder, Alexander Brown.

Book D, page 198. John Howell to Sampson Lanier for 500 pds 400 A in Rockingham & Guilford Counties on Troublesome Cr adj James Campbell, Burger Stone, William Thorp. June 7, 1795. A. Philips, Tho. Henderson.

Book D, page 199. William Fields to John Strong for 50 pds 50 A on Sharps Cr of Dan R adj Turbefield Barns, Thomas Henderson. Jan. 20, 1794. Joshua Smith, William Smith, John Smith.

Book D, page 200. John Lewis to Charles Dear for 25 pds 150 A on the Ride between Hogans Cr & Troublesome adj James Nickels, James McCaleb. 1794. John Nickels, Elizabeth Nickels.

Book D, page 201. Henry Pratt to John Thomas for 30 pds 100 A on Brushy fork of Jacobs Cr adj William Oldham Short, John Chadwell now William Farrar's line. Feb. 11, 1794. James Thomas, John Shepherd.

Book D, page 202. William Hunt of Person Co. to John Owen for 83 pds Va. money 408 A on both sides Town Cr adj Farley. Mar. 4, 1795. John Hunter, Jeremiah Norris.

Book D, page 203. Robert Gains of Charlotte Co., Va. to Thomas Brunt for 500 pds 380 A on S side Dan R adj Alexander McClaran. May 12, 1795. T. Searcy, Tho. Henderson.

Book D, page 204. John Davis & wife Ann to Thomas Fulford for 50 pds 74 A adj Thomas Sparks. Jan. 16, 1793. Sarah Potter, John Smith, Will. Bethell.

Book D, page 205. Richard Marr to Nicholas McCubbin for 100 pds 300 A on Wolf Island Cr. May 22, 1793. Wm. McCollum, Cornelus Dabney, John Challes.

Book D, page 206. George Thomas to Samuel Watt for 40 pds 66 A on Pruets fork of Hogans Cr adj Thomas Adams. Aug. 24, 1794. David Settle, Thomas Adams, Lovit Reed. (Lucie Thomas and Sarah Vaughan signed with George Thomas.)

Book D, page 207. County Court directs Abraham Philips, James Walker, John Dilworth, Joseph Payne and William Clark, Commissioners, to divide Real Estate of Joshua Wright dec'd. No. 1 Ester Pruet, widow of Joshua Wright dec'd, 302 A on Little Troublesome and Hogans Crs adj John Herrin & William Walker. No. 2 Jacob Wright 298 A on Hogans Cr adj Alexander Walker, Ridley, Hodge, Joseph Allen, Alexander Walker. No. 3 Josiah Wright 150 A on Giles Cr adj Hinson Humphrey. No. 4 William Wright 150 A on Giles Cr adj John Dilworth, No. 3, James Walker. Aug. 21, 1795. John Jones, Josiah Wright.

Book D, page 209. State of N.C. to Henry Pratt 100 A on Brushey Fork of Jacobs Cr adj John Shepherd, William Oldham Short, John Chadwell. June 27, 1793.

Book D, page 210. Moses Yell to William Elliott Sewter (also spelled Sutor) for 26 pds 18 sh 37 3/4 A on S side Gr Troublesome Cr adj John Waford, William Jones. Nov. 23, 1795. John Bawick, William Straton, John Suter.

Book D, page 211. Moses Yell to William Elliot Sewtor for 175 pds 113 A on both sides Gr Troublesome Cr adj Mateer, James McNealy. Nov. 11, 1795. John Bawick, John Sewter.

Book D, page 212. Moses Yell to William Elliot Sewtor for 50 pds 87 A on Gr Troublesome Cr adj Matear, James McNealy. Nov. 11, 1795. John Barwich, John Sewtor.

Book D, page 213. George Hornbuckle of Caswell Co. to William Hornbuckle for 30 pds 100 A on Country Line Cr adj Jeremiah Poston. Oct. 14, 1793. Henry Harden, Jeremiah Harden.

Book D, page 214. William Hornbuckle & wife Jane to Hugh Gwyn for 75 pds 100 A on Country Line Cr adj sd Gwyn, John Coxe, John Winsor. Nov. 17, 1794. Iverson Gwyn, Thomas Hornbuckle.

Book D, page 215. Thomas Mullin to William Mullen for 5 sh 290 A adj Ab. Benton. May 28,1795. David Settle, Carter Bethell, John Johnson.

Book D, page 216. William Hubbert to David Settle for 50 pds 47 A on Pruets fork of Hogans Cr adj sd Settle, sd Hubbert, Moses Garrison, Hugh Reed. May 22, 1794. John Matlock, George Hallum, Jere. Pritchet.

Book D, page 217. John Philips to Benjamin Moore for 25 pds 50 A on Hogans Cr adj sd Moore, Hodge, William Bradberry, William Harris. Oct. 14, 1795. Ezekiel Philips, Nancy Donnaky, Anna Donnaky, Tho. Thompson.

Book D, page 218. Isaac Kello to William Sillavant for 100 pds 100 A on Hogans Cr adj John Hodge. Nov. 26, 1795. A. Philips, John Odell.

Book D, page 219. Reuben Lowe & wife Mary to Isaac Kello for 100 pds 100 A on Hogans Cr adj Hodge, The Waggon Road. Aug. 14, 1793. A. Boyd, Thos. Lowe.

Book D, page 220. Joseph McCullock to Reuben Lowe for 100 pds 100 A on Hogans Cr and The Waggon Road. Feb. 5, 1793. A. Philips, Joseph McCullock.

Book D, page 221. William Case of Guilford to Charles Moore for 70 pds 136 A purchased from Nancy Mulloy, widow. Sept. 30, 1795. Richard Rosell, Ezekiel Frost.

Book D, page 222. James Campbell to James Whitsett for 50 pds 200 A on Big Troublesome Cr adj sd Campbell, John Howell Sr., being part of grant to Moses Campbell. Sept. 24, 1795. Thompson Lanier, Abner Bowen.

Book D, page 223. John Daniel Carner to George Brown for 50 pds 100 A on Troublesome Cr adj Thomas Lomzx, David Peeples. Nov. 26, 1793. Isaac Whitworth Jr.

Book D, page 224. Samuel Short to Moses Short for 50 pds 139 A on Jacobs Cr adj Charles Bruce. Sept. 22, 1794. John Shelton, Moses Short Sr., Moses Lomax.

Book D, page 225. John Stockird to William Asten Downey of Guilford Co. for 160 pds 284 A on both sides Rocky fork of Jacobs Cr adj Thomas Low, James Wright. Sept. 17, 1795. William Jones, Samuel Russell.

Book D, page 226. David Lovell to Robinson Ross 100 pds 200 A on Town Cr & Rockhouse Cr adj Thomas Norris. May 25, 1793. Richard Marr, John Jones.

Book D, page 227. Elijah West to James Davice for 25 pds 53 A on Gr Troublesome Cr adj Walter Martin, Robert Boak, being part of land layed off by A. Philips as directed by Commissioners Walter Martin, Robert Boak, Robert Bar, Soloman Webster for Elijah West orphan of Solomon West dec'd. Feb. 18, 1795. Walter Martin, Jonathon Hains.

Book D, page 228. John Dearing to Samuel Maxwell for 231 pds 5 sh 250 A on Big Troublesome Cr adj Thomas Lomax. Sept. 2, 1795. Charles Bruce, Joseph T. Joyce, Hubbard Peeples.

Book D, page 229. Joseph McGloughlen to Isham Simmons for 100 pds 100 A on Piney Fork. Nov. 3, 1794. John Simmons, Robert Lilley.

Book D, page 230. Alce (her mark) Nelson to William Godsey for 100 pds land on Jacobs Cr on which Alce Nelson now lives, for the term of her natural life, it being land retained as her right of dower when her son Thomas sold to James Lowe. Mar. 30, 1795. Tho. Henderson, Thos. Lowe, Robert Napier.

Book D, page 231. Ezekiel Callahan, Edward Callahan, Nathaniel Callahan, Jane Calahan, Darby Hopper, Jones Parrish and Unity Callahan to Robert Gilmore for 26 pds Va. money 53½ A on S side Matrimony Cr adj John Hopper. Nov. 29, 1794. John Gibson, Philip Rose, Jesse Harris.

Book D, page 232. Thomas Owen to John Harris for 50 pds 50 A adj John Smith. June 9, 1794. John Harris, Leaven Harris, William Atkins.

Book D, page 233. State of N.C. to Levy King 50 A on Big Troublesome Cr adj own land, Thomas Massey, John Baker. July 9, 1790.

Book D, page 234. Joseph Allen to John Payne for 100 pds 161 A on Hogans Cr adj sd Payne. Jan. 12, 1796. Joseph Clark, Nancy Clark.

Book D, page 235. State of N.C. to James Akin 200 A on Horse Pen Cr adj Bird, Coleman, Elisha Simmons. July 16, 1795.

Book D, page 236. State of N.C. to Benjamin McFarland 1,000 A in the Middle District on E side of Stones R. Dec. 17, 1794.

Book D, page 237. James Appleton & wife Margaret to John Winsor of Caswell Co. for $427 2/3 253 A on Countryline Cr adj Poston, Hornbuckle. Sept. 1, 1795.

Book D, page 238. Charles Moore to Isaac Periman for 35 pds 136 A on Richland Cr of How R, being land once granted to William Reves. Feb. 23, 1796. Robert Cummins, Jesse Rhodes.

Book D, page 239. Frederic William Marshall of Salem in Stokes Co. to Robert Williams for 283 pds 11 sh of hard money in gold and silver 212 A on Lickfork of Hogans Cr, being land in trust for Unitas Fratrum being deeded Apr. 20, 1764 from William Churton to Charles Metcalf and recorded in Orange Co. and Rowan Co. Sept. 12, 1795. Jacob B_____?, Lewis Meinung, Duke Williams.

Book D, page 240. James Hunter to William, Nicholas, Samuel, John and Ual (Ewell) Dalton, Heirs of Samuel Dalton (Jr.) dec'd for 250 pds Va. currency 630 A on Bever Island Cr adj upper line of sd Hunter. Aug. 28, 1793. Ack in Open Court by W. Bethell.

Book D, page 241. Thomas Lovens of Stokes Co. to William Ward for 20 pds 200 A on Beaver Island Cr adj Joseph Reed, Stokes Co. line, James Hunter, Archibald Hughes. Aug. 4, 1792. James Hunter, James Callaham.

Book D, page 242. State of N.C. to Ezekiel Curry 32 A on Haw R adj William Metair, John McKibbin. Nov. 17, 1790.

Book D, page 243. Joseph Cloud Thrasher & wife Margaret to Acquilla Wilson for 275 pds Va. money 831 A on Lickfork of Hogans Cr adj William Bethell, John Thrasher. Dec. 4, 1795. A. Philips, Aq. Wilson Jr.

Book D, page 244. James McCaleb to Leaven Woolen for $600.00 300 A on both sides Little Troublesome Cr adj Andrew Boyd, James Nicols, being part of grant to Catharine McCaleb. Oct. 28, 1795. A. Philips, John Harris, Thomas North.

Book D, page 245. John Horsford & wife Elizabeth to James Hays for 79 pds 77 A on Hogans Cr. May 15, 1795. Obadiah Howerton, _____ Chapman.

Book D, page 246. John Hunter to William Norris for 15 pds 366 A on Little Town Cr and a br of Wolf Island Cr adj Coalson Porter. Jan. 26, 1796. William Stephens, Courtney Norman, Jarrat Nelson.

Book D, page 247. Robert Martin to James Philips for 50 pds 106½ A on Wolf Island Cr adj Samuel Herrin, John Covinton, Patrick Wardlow. Nov. 16, 1793. William Martin, Baily Martin.

Book D, page 248. Nathaniel Linder to William Eagle of Guilford Co. for 25 pds 50 A on Jacobs Cr adj James Wright, William Asten Downey, Richard Hingson. Sept. 18, 1795. James Harkins, Samuel Trolinger.

Book D, page 249. Jacob Cantrill to Henry Kilman for 10 pds 25A on Wolf Island Cr adj sd Cantrill, Cummings. Feb. 26, 1796. Aaron Cantril, Edward Woolen.

Book D, page 250. Talitha Browder to Asa Cummins for 100 pds 640 A on Wolf Island Cr adj James Cantrell. Nov. 9, 1795. John Browder, Cloud Thrasher.

Book D, page 251. James Daniel to Henry Kilman for 100 pds 153 A on Wolf Island Cr adj Jacob Cantrell, Elijah Cantrell. Feb. 27, 1796. B. C. Lacy, A. Philips.

Book D, page 252. John Bell Jr. of Washington Co. to Sutton McCollister for 50 pds 200 A on Wolf Island Cr. & Bold Run Cr adj John Perkle. Sept. 12, 1794. James McCarrell, Caty Brandon.

Book D, page 253. John Payne & wife Elizabeth to Richard Thomas for 100 pds 200 A on Londons Cr of Wolf Island Cr. Dec. 7, 1795. Patrick Twomey (?), Coleson Porter, Lawrence Porter.

Book D, page 254. James Williams to James Asbridge for 37 pds 10 sh 55 A on Wolf Island Cr adj Elisha Barnard, Elijah Cantrell, Thomas Pound. Feb. 25, 1796. Benjamin Williams, Jacob Cantrell.

Book D, page 255. William Allen & wife Agnes of Grayson Co., Va. to Joseph Allen for 156 pds 200 A on Grammers Br of Pruets Fork adj Josiah Settle, Thomas McCullock. Jan. 9, 1796. Samuel Allen, John McCay, John Denny.

Book D, page 256. George Rowland to Emanuel James for 137 pds 137 A on Haw R adj Michael Caffey, being land whereon Rowland lives. Jan. 16, 1796. John Wafford, John Gardner.

Book D, page 257. John Joyce to Thomas Joyce for 200 pds 200 A
on N side Mayo R. Feb. 13, 1796. Robert Joyce, Elijah Joyce,
Thos. Joyce.

Book D, page 258. State of N.C. to James Hays Jr. 150 A on
Jacobs Cr adj John D. Carner, Jacob Whitworth, Pleasant Henderson.
July 16, 1795.

Book D, page 259. State of N.C. to James Hays 100 A on Jacobs
Cr adj Alexander Martin Esq, John D. Carner. July 16, 1795.

Book D, page 260. State of N.C. to Alexander Sneed 200 A on
Buffalo Island Cr adj Grogan. July 16, 1795.

Book D, page 261. State of N.C. to Robert Small 200 A on Piney
Fork adj William Miller, Benjamin Hoggard. May 16, 1787.

Book D, page 262. State of N.C. to Robert Small on both sides
Piney Cr adj sd Small, William Miller. May 16, 1787.

Book D, page 263. State of N.C. to Robert Small 100 A on Big
Troublesome Cr adj William Miller. July 9, 1794.

Book D, page 264. State of N.C. to Robert Boak 60 A on Big
Troublesome Cr adj John Wafford, William Jones, James McNealy,
Moses Yell. July 9, 1794.

Book D, page 265. State of N.C. to James McCarrell 100 A on Gr
Rockhouse Cr adj James Brown, William Baker, Joseph Cunningham.
June 27, 1793.

Book D, page 268. State of N.C. to John Smith 100 A on Wolf
Island Cr adj William Russell, James Hopwood. July 16, 1795.

Book D, page 269. Thomas Owens to Leven Harris for $57.00 50 A
on Hogans Cr adj John Harris. Mar. 1796. Thomas North, William
Harris, Mary Bateman.

Book D, page 270. John Oliver to James Oliver 200 A on upper
Hogans Cr. (Date and price omitted.) W. Bethell.

Book D, page 271. Isaac Lowe Sr. to Daniel Deanes, John Lewis,
Thomas Thompson, George Dilworth, William Jones Sr. & John
Pearson, Trustees for 10 sh 1 A on which Lowes Meeting House now
stands, for the only use of Methodist Episcopal Church. Mar. 25,
1796. John Averet, Thomas Gutry, James Hodge.

Book D, page 272. James McCarrel to Robert Boak for 50 pds 100
A on Gr Rockhouse Cr adj William Baker, Joseph Cunningham. Feb.
24, 1796. Israel McCarrell, Tennen More.

Book D, page 273. Thomas King Sr. to John King for 50 pds 100 A
on Gr Troublesome Cr adj Alexander Brown, Moses Short. May 24,
1796. W. Bethell.

Book D, page 274. State of N.C. to Pleasant Henderson 100 A adj
Alexander Martin Esqr. July 9, 1794.

Book D, page 275. Ezekiel Curry to Daniel Deane for 150 pds 150
A on S side Haw R adj Peter Merselit. April 20, 1796. A.
Philips, William Jones, Robert Curry.

Book D, page 276. Benjamin Settle & wife Mary to Josiah Settle
for 40 pds 20 A. Apr. 19, 1796. David Settle, John Matlock,
Edward Settle.

Book D, page 277. Benjamin Settle & wife Mary to Josiah Settle
for 40 pds 100 A adj John Matlock. Apr. 19, 1796. David Settle,
John Matlock, Edward Settle.

Book D, page 278. Aaron Allen to Robert Boak for 50 pds 96 A on
Big Troublesome Cr adj James McCarrell, James Brown, Thomas King,
John Young. Mar. 9, 1796. John Fields, R. Galloway.

Book D, page 279. State of N.C. to Francis McBride 25 A on Big
Troublesome Cr adj own land, James Flack. June 27, 1793.

Book D, page 280. State of N.C. to Alexander Martin 640 A on
Jacobs Cr adj Michael Trolinger, Sutton McCollister, John Cummins,
Alexander Brown. July 9, 1794.

Book D, page 281. State of N.C. to Bryant Thomas 150 A on Sharps
Cr adj Lewis Thomas, Turbyfield Barnes (formerly John Gann),
Richard Vernon. Dec. 20, 1791.

Book D, page 282. State of N.C. to Alexander Martin 150 A on
Jacobs Cr adj Andrew Conners, Samuel Short. July 16, 1795.

Book D, page 283. George Summers of Caswell Co. to Dennis Kelly
for 100 pds 288 A in Sumner Co. on N side of Smiths Fork adj
James Andrew. June 6, 1796. George Wilson, Ligah Loyd, Jas.
Somers.

Book D, page 284. William Hornbuckle & wife Jane to Cagebeth
White of Mecklenburg Co. for 225 pds 225 A on Country Line Cr
adj Thomas Hardin, Hugh Gwyn, George Hornbuckle. Nov. 16, 1795.
John White, William Edward, Howard Cash.

Book D, page 285. Joseph Garner to John Watt for 250 pds 315 A
on Hogans Cr and the Cabban Br adj sd Garner, James Dyer. 1795.
Saml. Watt, James Watt.

Book D, page 286. William Thornton Morton to Susanna Marr, Adm
of John Marr dec'd of Henry Co., Va. for 100 pds 300 A on E side
Dan R on Hunters Mill Road, being land granted in 1783 to James
Roberts. May 26, 1796. Richard Bethell.

Book D, page 287. Leonard Barker to Peter Wilson for 200 pds
30 A on Mayo R adj Thomas Joyce, William Beaver, Thomas Henderson. May 9, 1796. Sam. Henderson, William McCollum.

Book D, page 288. A. Philips resurveys and divides 819 A of
John Curry dec'd for Division of Estate among children. No. 1
Ezekiel Curry 150 A on Haw R. No. 2 John Curry 175 A on N side
Haw R adj John Mateer. No. 3 Moses Curry 183 A on Haw R. No. 4
Robert Curry 97 A on Haw R. No. 5 Ezekiel Curry & Susanna Curry
53 A. No. 6 Jean Irvin 78 A. No. 7 Susanna Curry 78½ A. No.
8 Robert Curry 4 A.

Book D, page 291. William Beavers & wife Abigail to Peter Wilson for 30 pds 6 A on Mayo R adj sd Beaver & sd Wilson, Galloway, Henderson. May 23, 1796. William McClellen.

Book D, page 292. Nehemiah Vernon, John McCune & Sarah McCune to Bird Deatheridge for 50 pds Va. money 50 A adj Joshua Smith, John Mathis. Jan. 25, 1795. Turbafield Barns, Robert Joyce, Mathew Peggs.

Book D, page 293. Benjamin Smith to Benjamin Smith Jr. for 20 pds 40 A on Mayo R adj Virginia line. May 23, 1796. Daniel Grogan, William Grogan.

Book D, page 294. Richard Marr to William Hickman for 30 pds 64 A. Oct. 11, 1795. Duke Williams, Willie Pound (?).

Book D, page 295. Gift Deed of William Thomas to Sarah Lewis in consideration of love & her better maintainance 150 A on Sharps Cr adj Lewis Thomas, Turbyfield Barns, Richard Vernon, line of Charles Galloway dec'd. Feb. 22, 1796. Nehemiah Vernon, Mary Vernon, Sarah Sims Vernon.

Book D, page 296. Aniel Fields to Joseph Odell for 20 pds 100 A adj Benjamin Smith, Drury Smith. May 23, 1796. Nehemiah Vernon, Mary Vernon, Sary Sims Vernon.

Book D, page 297. Isham Sharp to Richard Sharp for 500 pds proclamation money 228 A on S side Mayo R adj Joshua Smith, James Cook. May 19, 1796. Watson Gentry, William Cardwell, James Scales.

Book D, page 298. Robert Martin to John Hamilton for 100 pds 298 A on Piney Cr adj Robert Boak. May 1796. Robt. Boak, William Boak.

Book D, page 299. David Rowland to Benjamin Webb for 137 pds 137 A on Haw R adj James Wright, Christopher Vandegraph, William Jones, being part of tract unto John Rowland from Estate of George Rowland dec'd & then conveyed to David Rowland. Feb. 13, 1796. Thomas Webb, A. Boyd.

Book D, page 300. David Rowland to Benjamin Webb for 137 pds 137 A on Haw R adj James Wright, William Jones, John Sprout, being tract laid out unto sd David Rowland from Estate of George Rowland dec'd. Feb. 13, 1796. Thomas Webb, A. Boyd.

Book D, page 301. James Martin of Stokes Co. to Pleasant Henderson for 400 pds 1,000 A on Upper Hogans Cr & Dan R. May 31, 1795. Samuel Henderson.

Book D, page 302. Pleasant Henderson to Alexander Martin Esq for 100 pds 640 A on Jacobs Cr adj Charles Bruce. Oct. 8, 1794. David Walker, T. Searcy.

Book D, page 303. Robert Crump of Stokes Co. to Thomas Asher for 10 pds 50 A on Bever Island Cr adj Stokes Co. line, Dearing, Henderson, Thomas Loven. Aug. 22, 1796. William Crump, John Vawters, George Joyce.

Book D, page 304.   Joshua Smith Esq, Sheriff, to John Peay 790 A
on S & E sides of Dan R for 450 pds, being part of Est of Cyrus
L. Roberts dec'd seized by order of William Bethell, C.C., and
sold to highest bidder to satisfy debts to John Cox esq, John
Lemon Sr., Elizabeth Roberts, Vanlandingham for Galloway Co.
May 4, 1796.   Alex. McClaran, Vincent Wheeler.

Book D, page 305.   Robert Hatrick to Robert Donaldson for 69 pds
46 A adj James Taylor, Andrew Wilson.   Aug. 25, 1796.   W. Nash,
Will Bethell.

Book D, page 306.   Aaron Allen to John Baker Jr. for 50 pds 100
A on Rockhouse Cr adj Job Baker, William Baker, William Pursell.
Mar. 1, 1796.   Job Baker, William Baker, William Jones.

Book D, page 307.   James Rhodes to William Thomas for 10 pds
proclamation money 150 A adj former tract of John Gann but now
Turbefield Barnes, Charles Galloway dec'd, Richard Vernon.   Jan.
25, 1796.   Nehemiah Vernon, Obadiah Vernon, John Vernon.

Book D, page 308.   John Joyce to Samuel Sharp for 25 pds Va.
money 200 A on Mayo R adj James Belton, Richard Cardwell.   Jan.
4, 1793.   Nehemiah Vernon, William Joyce, Alexander Joyce.

Book D, page 309.   Thomas Massey to Nathan Massey for 50 pds 178
A on N side Big Troublesome Cr adj sd Thomassey, John Baker,
Alexander Brown.   1796.   Edward R. Peebles, James Martin.

Book D, page 310.   John Leak Esq to Robert Coleman for 400 pds
300 A on N side Dan R adj Bazley Bourne, Joseph Parker, John
Menzie.   May 28, 1796.   Jno. Peay, Thomas Peay, John Lemon Jr.

Book D, page 311.   Robert Axton to Nusham Barham for 100 pds 175
A on E side Mayo R.   July 30, 1796.   Joshua Smith, Robt. Joyce,
John Smith.

Book D, page 312.   David Barnard to John Sims for 150 pds 150 A
on Dan R.   Aug. 24, 1796.   Richard Bethell.

Book D, page 313.   George Kimble to Jacob Bernard for 50 pds 12
A on Wolf Island Cr adj John Walker.   May 1795.   Nathl. Linder,
Wm. Southerland.

Book D, page 314.   Abner Parrott to Drury Smith for 10 pds 33 A.
Aug. 22, 1796.   Peter Williams, Sally Williams.

Book D, page 315.   William Stratton to Duncan Beith for 30 pds
50 A on Little Troublesome Cr adj James Nickels, being land sd
Stratton bought of Isaac Condley.   Oct. 30, 1795.   A. Philips,
James Sprout.

Book D, page 316.   James Saunders to Heirs of John Marr dec'd for
67 pds 260 A on Gr Rockhouse & Piney Crs adj John McCarrell, John
Perkle, being land granted unto sd James Saunders from aforesaid
estate.   1796.

Book D, page 317.   James Saunders to James Saunders Jr. for 67
pds 83 A on Gr Rockhouse Cr adj Benjamin Haggard, William Miller,
Abraham Philips. Aug. 26, 1796.   A. Philips, John Hunter.

Book D, page 318.   Thomas Scott to Walter Hill for 10 pds 40 A
on Benajah Cr adj sd Hill. Nov.29,1790. A.Philips, Edw.Williams,
Robt.Boak.

Book D, page 319. John Harper to John Hartford Taylor for 10 pds 29½ A on E side Mill Cr adj Gwyn. July 27, 1795. A. Philips, Jonathon Haines, James Garner.

Book D, page 320. Salathem Newnam to John Horford Taylor for 60 pds 100 A on Mill Cr. July 27, 1795. A. Philips, Jonathon Haines, John Harper.

Book D, page 321. Ezekiel Curry & Susanna Curry to William Jones Jr. for $106.00 53 A adj sd Jones, Moses Curry, Robert Curry, being part of tract left to James Curry dec'd and on his death became property of Ezekiel & Susanna Curry. Apr. 20, 1796. A. Philips, Daniel Deanes, John Bennett.

Book D, page 322. Robert Martin to Samuel Herron for 50 pds 106½ A on Wolf Island Cr adj sd Herron, Abraham Philips. Aug. 7, 1794. John Harper, Elijah Baker.

Book D, page 323. Willis Pruet & wife Hester to Andrew Boyd for 150 pds 300 A on both sides Dixie Road adj James Allen, Estate of Joshua Wright dec'd, being land alloted to sd Hest Pruet who was former wife of sd Joshua Wright. Apr. 12, 1796. Josiah Wright, Joshua Pruet.

Book D, page 324. Walter Hill to William Cartwright for 10 pds 154 A on Haw R adj John Caffey, Campbell. Aug. 29, 1793. James Stewart, John Woffard.

Book D, page 325. Walter Hill to William Cartwright for 10 pds 40 A on Benajah Cr. Aug. 29, 1793. James Stewart, John Wofford.

Book D, page 326. State of N.C. to Philip Anglen 189 A on N side Mayo R on Virginia line adj William Kellam, Joel Gibson, Lambath Dotson. May 16, 1787.

Book D, page 327. State of N.C. to Levi King 200 A on Jacobs Cr adj Alexander Martin, Joseph Cunningham, Michael Trolinger, Sutton McCollister. July 16, 1795.

Book D, page 328. Thomas McCullough to William Philips for 100 pds 160 A on Hogans Cr adj sd Philips. Oct. 27, 1794. John Philips, William Philips.

Book D, page 329. State of N.C. to Thomas Raffety 150 A on Wolf Island Cr adj William Bethell, Leaven Mitchel, Isaac Cantrill. July 16, 1795.

Book D, page 330. State of N.C. to Thomas Raferty 200 A on Town Cr adj Alem B. Williams, Leaven Mitchel. July 16, 1795.

Book D, page 331. Thomas Lee Shippen & wife Elizabeth Carter of Philadelphia, Pa. grant Power of Atty to James Taylor to superintend the land of Hon. Francis Farley Esq late of Island of Antigua, Privy Counseller dec'd, in Rockingham & Caswell Counties which was left by his will to his grand daus. Elizabeth Carter

Shippen, Maria Carter, Mary Byrd Farley and Rebecca Park Corbin.
May 27, 1796. W. Shippen Jr., Alexander Martin.

Book D, page 333. Alexander Joyce Esq, High Sheriff, to William
Lacy for 7 pds 10 sh 640 A adj sd Lacy, George Judge, Robert
Goins, being land seized by order of Court for debt of Nicholas
Larimore and recovered by Robert Goins. Jan. 23, 1795. Alex.
McClaran, Elias Peay, Robt. Brown.

Book D, page 334. William Lacy to William Farrar for 40 pds 640
A adj sd Lacy, George Judge, Robert Goins. Apr. 3, 1795. Tho.
Henderson, Alex. Joyce, Sam. Henderson.

Book D, page 335. Sarah Odineal, John Odineal & Tate Odineal,
Heirs of John Odineal to Isaac Clark in obedience of the Court
of Equity for District of Salisbury 244 A on Wolf Island Cr.
Nov. 16, 1796. A. Philips, W. McCollum.

Book D, page 336. Joshua Smith, High Sheriff, to William Cochran
and William Hubbert for 30 pds 13 sh 219 A on Pruets of Hogans
Cr adj Josiah Settle, David Vaughan, being land seized by order
of Court of Caswell Co. to be sold to highest bidder to satisfy
debt of Josiah Mann as recovered by Holland Sumner. Oct. 20,
1796. Samuel Shelton, John Smith, Joseph Shelton.

Book D, page 337. William Hubert, William Cochran & Reubin
Cochran to David Benton for 50 pds 100 A on Pruits fork of Hogans Cr adj Josiah Settle, David Settle, Solomon Loftist's old
boundary line, Vaughan Williams. Oct. 25, 1796. Robert Williams,
Duke Williams.

BOOK E

Book E, page 1. Isaac Lowe to John Atkins for 67 pds 10 sh or
$135.00 157 A where I moved from unless the sd Lowe or Heirs pay
67 pds, 10 sh or $135.00 to John Atkins on or before June 15.
Dec. 20, 1795. Robert Williams.

Book E, page 2. Isaac Lowe to Simon Swail of the Town of Petersburg for 75 pds Va. money 157 A on Little Troublesome & Hogans Cr.
adj William Walker, Thomas Conner. Jan.5,1796. John Browder,
Isham Browder.

Book E, page 3. State of N.C. to Abraham Philips and William
Bethell 175 A on Fishing Cr adj sd Philips & Bethell, Charles
Galloway, Peter Duncan. July 16, 1795.

Book E, page 4. State of N.C. to Abraham Philips & William
Bethell 200 A on Fishing Cr & Town Cr and Sarra Town Road adj sd
Philips & Bethell, David Lovelle, Edward Williams, Peter Duncan.
July 16, 1795.

Book E, page 5. Isaac Clark Esq, High Sheriff, to John Hunter
for 35 pds 12 sh 168 A on Guilford Co. line adj Joshua Caffey,
being land seized by order of Guilford Co. Court and sold to
highest bidder on Jan. 28, 1789 to satisfy debt of John Odineal
as recovered by Manlove Torrant. (Signer is recorded as Isaac
Clark, late Sheriff.) Joseph Clark, John Coffee. Sept. 1,1796.

Book E, page 6. John Hunter to Joshua Coffee for 50 pds 168 A
on Haw R adj Guilford Co. line. Sept. 10, 1796. Richd. Marr,
Jno. Coffee.

Book E, page 7. Joshua Coffee to James Averet for 233 pds 203 A on Haw R & Kennedy Br adj Guilford Co. line, Daugherty, William Wright, Henry Brannock. Nov.25,1796. A. Philips, John Dougherty.

Book E, page 8. James Caruthers to Philip Gates for 25 pds 200 A on Brushy fork of Hogans Cr adj sd Gates, Jacob Whitworth. Dec. 27, 1790. James Hays Sr., James Hays Jr.

Book E, page 9. William Young to Annanias Green for 50 pds 100 A on Wolf Island Cr adj Jarrot Brandon, John Bell, Elijah Cantrell, John McCarrell. Mar. 15, 1796. William Brown, Ezekiel Wright, James Lord.

Book E, page 10. Sutton McCollister to Annanies Green for 50 pds 55 A on Wolf Island Cr adj William Young. Mar. 10, 1796. William Brown, James Lord, Ezekiel Wright.

Book E, page 11. James Martin to James Delay for 50 pds 100 A on N side Haw R, being part of 490 A grant in 1779 to sd Martin. Nov. 5, 1784. A. Philips, Hezekiah Rhodes, Andrew Wittie.

Book E, page 12. William Clark to Levice Allen for 50 pds 56 A in two tracts on Pruets Fork adj John Matlock, Samuel Watt, Widow Allen, James Hodge. Nov.17,1796. Joseph Clark, Nancy Clark.

Book E, page 13. James Strange to Fanny Strange for 5 sh 100 A on Billews Cr. Nov. 26, 1796. Joseph Ladd, Joshua Young, Elijah Wright.

Book E, page 14. Mary Patrick to James Patrick for 20 pds 189 A on Mill Cr adj both parties, George Martin, Benjamin Dilworth. Aug. 25, 1794. Samuel McSparan, Mathew Covey.

Book E, page 15. Henry Grogan to William Hopper for 28 pds 100 A on Little Buffalo of Matrimony Cr adj sd Hopper & Grogan. Mar. 28, 1796. Joseph Hopper, Jesse Hinton.

Book E, page 16. James Lomax of S.C. to William Ferrington of Guilford Co. for 50 pds 200 A on Hogans and Jacobs Crs & both sides Johnson King's old Road. Sept. 24, 1787. Thomas Lomax, Lomax, Gardner.

Book E, page 17. Nathan Cardwell to Joel Mackey for 50 pds 100 A on Mirey Br adj sd Mackey. Oct. 22, 1796. Nehemiah Vernon, Nicholas Dalton, Samuel Dalton.

Book E, page 18. Thomas King to Lemire King for 20 pds 60 A on Gr Rockhouse Cr adj Allen Williams, Thomas Larkin, being land bought of John Perkle. Aug.28,1794. Nathal. Linder, Peter Watson.

Book E, page 19. James Brown to Samuel Brown for 80 pds 100 A on Gr Troublesome Cr adj Richard Henderson, being part of tract James Brown bought from his father James Brown Sr. dec'd. Oct. 20, 1794. Aaron Allen, Robert Brown.

Book E, page 20. Mary Linder, late __?__ of Nathaniel Linder dec'd to Samuel Trolinger for 10 pds 250 A on Jacobs Cr adj Richard Hingson, William Downey. Nov. 29, 1796. A. Philips, Vincent Wheeler.

Book E, page 21. William Johnson to John Saunders for 100 pds 125 A on Wolf Island Cr adj Patrick Wardlow, William Spiers former line, now John Harrises, Browder. Oct. 13, 1796. A. Philips.

Book E, page 22. Abraham Womack, Atty for Humphry Garrett, to Edward Thompson for 50 pds 100 A on Burchfield fork of Wolf Island Cr adj Richard Marr. Jan. 31, 1793. William Bethell, Josiah Womack, John Womack.

Book E, page 23. Charles Baker to John Baker for 100 pds 128 A on fork of Big Troublesome Cr adj Thomas Massey, Thomas Henderson, James Brown. Oct. 30, 1795. Job Baker, Aaron Allen, William Jones.

Book E, page 24. John Harmon, commonly called Watson, and wife Sarah to Adam Crawford for 20 pds 100 A on Belues Cr adj Isaac Whitworth, Robert Dearing, being a grant to sd John Harmon registered in Guildord Co. Feb. 26, 1794. William Harden, Sydwell Watkins, William Dearing. (Signed John Watson, Sarah Watson.)

Book E, page 25. Robert Boak to James Hamilton for 100 pds 137 A on Troublesome Cr adj Andrew Martin, Widow West, Hugh Lynch. Sept. 23, 1796. William Boak, Stephen Hamilton.

Book E, page 26. George Rowland to Thomas Stokes of Guilford Co. for 50 pds 100 A on Gr Rockhouse Cr adj Robert Walker, Charles Mitchel, Isaac Philips. March 1796. Jno. Coffee.

Book E, page 27. Laurence Bankson to Edward Woolen for 100 pds 175 A on both sides Wolf Island Cr adj William Daniel, Asa Cummings, Henry Kilman, Isaac Cantril. Oct. 7, 1796. Jacob Cantrill, Henry Kilman.

Book E, page 28. John Watt to Ezekiel Jones for 100 pds 200 A on Pruets Cr of Hogans Cr adj Hannah Harris, Nathan Thacker, William Obanion, being tract entered by Zachariah Thacker and surveyed by Abraham Philips. Nov. 20, 1795. Saml. Watt, Charles Dean, John Mathews.

Book E, page 29. Jeremiah Thacker & wife Mary Ann to Charles Thacker for 50 pds 100 A on Hogans Cr adj sd Charles Thacker, Benjamin Moore. Oct. 1, 1796. David Settle, Usler Thacker.

Book E, page 30. Gift Deed of John Mount to Thomas Mount for & in consideration of love and affection & for 10 sh 125 A on both sides Chambers Mill Road adj lands of Benton, Smith & Hickman. Apr. 11, 1796. Robert Williams, Humphry Mount.

Book E, page 32. Gift Deed of John Mount to Humphry Mount for & in consideration of love & affection and for 10 sh 125 A on Chambers Mill Rd. Apr. 11, 1796. Robert Williams, Thomas Mount.

Book E, page 33. James Goings to Thomas Henderson for 100 pds (no description). Oct. 6, 1786. Joshua Smith, Turbyfield Barns, James Pratt.

Book E, page 34. State of N.C. to Henry Scales 200 A on Buffalo Cr. July 16, 1795.

Book E, page 35. State of N.C. to Henry Scales 100 A on Buffalo Island Cr adj Alexander Sneed, John Hill. Dec. 20, 1796.

Book E, page 36. State of N.C. to Hugh Linch 270 A on Big Troublesome Cr adj Richard Rossel, James Frost, Mary Patrick, William Buckanon. July 16, 1795.

Book E, page 37. State of N.C. to Hugh Linch 28 A on Big Troubles Cr adj sd Linch, Robert Small. Sept. 20, 1797.

Book E, page 38. State of N.C. to David Barnard 50 A on Still House Cr adj sd Barnard, Joel Watkins, Thomas Henderson. Dec. 20, 1796.

Book E, page 39. State of N.C. to Frederich Ford 40 A on Jacobs Cr adj sd Ford, George Ford, James Hays Jr. July 16, 1795.

Book E, page 40. State of N.C. to Nathaniel Harris 60 A on S side Matrimony Cr adj sd Harris. Dec. 20, 1796.

Book E, page 41. State of N.C. to William Cannon 50 A on Jacobs Cr adj John Shepherd, Jacob Whitworth, Abraham Whitworth, Henry Pratt. July 16, 1795.

Book E, page 42. State of N.C. to John & William Conner 50 A on Jacobs Cr adj Samuel Short, John Cunningham, Cumings, Martin, Soloman Hopkins. July 16, 1795.

Book E, page 43. State of N.C. to William Conner 73 A on Jacobs Cr adj Samuel Short. July 16, 1795.

Book E, page 44. John Chadwell, planter to William Farrar for 100 pds 400 A on Brushey fork of Jacobs Cr adj Martha Caruthers now Philip Gates line. Mar. 13, 1793. Alex. Martin, Thomas Rogers.

Book E, page 45. Thomas Bernard & wife Agnes to Shadrack Yeoman for 40 pds 52 A on Little Rockhouse Cr adj sd Bernard. Aug. 10, 1792. A. Philips, John Strange, Stokes Yeoman, Joseph Garner.

Book E, page 46. Joseph Payne & wife Martha to William Wright for 50 pds 250 A on Hogans & Troublesome Crs adj James Allen. May 26, 1794. Alexander Walker, William Hodge, Joseph Allen.

Book E, page 47. Joseph Payne & wife Martha to Jacob Wright for 30 pds 44 A on Troublesome Cr adj John Allen, John Herring. May 26, 1794. Alexander Walker, William Hodge, Joseph Allen.

Book E, page 48. Henry King to Thomas King Jr. for 100 pds 200 A on both sides Gr Rockhouse Cr adj David Purswell, Robert Small, Abraham Philips, being early land grant to John Young. Dec. 30, 1790. A. Philips, Robt. Brown, John Conner.

Book E, page 49. John Young to Thomas King Jr. for 10 pds 60 A on Gr Rockhouse Cr adj Robert Small. Jan. 3, 1791. A. Philips, Richard Kingson, William Nance.

Book E, page 50. State of N.C. to William Fanning 50 A on Buffalo Island Cr adj sd Fanning, Allen Dodd. Dec. 20, 1796.

Book E, page 51. Thomas Wilson to Benjamin Settle for 200 pds 154 A on 2 brs of Pruets fork of Hogans Cr adj Josiah Settle, John & Thomas Wilson. Aug. 25, 1795. David Settle, Daniel Allen, Joseph Reed, John Reed.

Book E, page 52. William Philips to Sarah Wheeler for 140 pds 242 A on Hogans Cr adj Walker. Jan. 24, 1797. V. Wheeler, E. Wheeler.

Book E, page 53. Bryant Senior to Joseph Scott for 100 pds 91 A on Hogans Cr adj Thomas Parks. Mar. 25, 1795. William Bethell, Richard Bethell, Robert Mullin.

Book E, page 54. Stokely Donelson of Knoxville, Tenn. to John C. Cox for 50 pds 640 A in Davidson Co., Tenn. on Spring Cr, a fork of Sycamore Cr adj Samuel Morsour, Nehemiah Long, being land granted by State of N.C. to Samuel Marsour, Assignee of Howell Underwood by Grant No. 906 dated 1789. Dec. 24, 1796. P. H. Fountain, N. Williams Jr.

Book E, page 55. Asa Brasher to Zaza Brasher for 30 pds 60 A on N side Jacobs Cr. May 7, 1791. Thomas Knight.

Book E, page 56. Michael Leathers & wife to John Payne for $125.00 100 A on Hogans Cr. Nov. 19, 1796. J. Williams, Isaac Payne, Joseph Clark.

Book E, page 57. William Taylor to Bailey Martin for 50 pds 94 A on Hogans Cr adj sd Martin, John Thompson, Gentry Thompson. May 23, 1796. William Stapleton, Hortford Taylor, Jesse Kerr.

Book E, page 58. John Thompson to Bailey Martin for 5 pds 100 A on Hogans Cr adj sd Thompson, Henry Sanders, Horford Taylor. Oct. 16, 1795. James Taylor.

Book E, page 59. Andrew Wray to William Martin for 50 pds 50 A on Little Troublesome Cr adj sd Wray, Robert Wray. Feb. 28, 1797.

Book E, page 60. Gift Deed of Elizabeth Strong to son John Strong 2 featherbeds, 2 heifers, 8 hogs. Feb. 24, 1797. Frederich Irion, Richard Vernon.

Book E, page 61. David Dolton of Stokes Co. to Isaac Dolton of Stokes for 10 pds 100 A on Pappaw Cr adj Drury Smith, Samuel Dolton, Joshua Mabry. Apr. 1795. Alex Joyce, John Bostick, John Fendel Carr.

Book E, page 63. William Baker & wife Amey to John Watt for 100 pds 180 A on Vaughans Cr of Hogans Cr adj Charles Dean, Obanion. Feb. 28, 1792. Saml. Watt, Ezekiel Jones.

Book E, page 64. Aaron Allen to John Smith for 50 pds land on Brushey Fork of Gr Rockhouse Cr adj sd Allen, Job Baker, William Jones, Joseph Cunningham. Mar. 16, 1796. Ben Polk, James Saunders.

Book E, page 65. James Nickels to John Nickels for 50 pds 155 A on Little Troublesome Cr adj William Stratton, James McCaleb, Charles Deer. Oct. 29, 1795. A. Philips, William Conner.

Book E, page 66. John Leak Esq to Richard Stewart of Petersburg, Va. for $20.00 ½ A in Town of Leaksville, corner of Henry St. & Water St. Feb. 16, 1797. P. Garland, R. Garland, Jas. Parks.

Book E, page 67. William Case to Ben Dawson Smith for 50 pds

100 A on Haw R. Feb. 25, 1797. James Russey, Sarah Russey, Jonas Frost.

Book E, page 68. David Lovell to James Fletcher of Wilks Co. for 67.2.8 67 A adj Parker. May 14, 1796. George Jones, John Simmons, Zachariah Lovell.

Book E, page 69. David Lovell to James Fletcher of Wilks Co. for 100 pds 133 A on N side Town Cr adj Joseph Patten, William Hunt, Robert Hudson. May 14, 1796. Geo Jones, John Simmons, Zach. Lovell.

Book E, page 70. David Lovell to James Fletcher of Wilks for 100 pds 200 A on Town Cr adj Sarah Potter John Simmons, Zach. Lovell.

Book E, page 71. Drury Williams & Aron Williams to Robert Galloway for 200 pds Va. money 345 A on Big Rockhouse & Bare Swamp adj sd Galloway, Claiborne Wall, the road from Eagle Falls to the Courthouse. Dec. 19, 1796. A. Philips, Peter Watson.

Book E, page 72. Thomas Scott to Stephen Stacy for $202.00 101 A on Bennajah Cr adj John Waford, William Cartwright, John Dougherty, Caffey. Mar. 1, 1796. A. Philips, John Daugherty.

Book E, page 73. Samuel Allen of Buckingham Co., Va. & Vallentine Allen Jr. to Robert Galloway for 320 pds Va. money 300 A on the River adj Vallentine Allen Sr. Jan. 14, 1797. John Menzies, James Scales, Samuel Allen, George Barnes.

Book E, page 74. Thomas Grogan to George Coulson for 50 pds 100 A on Fishing Cr. Oct. 5, 1795. Nehemiah Vernon, James Rhodes, Richard Grogan.

Book E, page 75. Samuel Calhoun of Guilford Co. to Andrew & Thomas Lewis for 16 pds 200 A on Hogans Cr adj Thomas Bowen, Michael Thomas, Benjamin Bowen. Feb. 25, 1797. John Hamilton, Arthur Reynell.

Book E, page 76. Philip Anglen of Henry Co., Va. to Benjamin Smith Jr. for 50 pds 55 A on N side Mayo R. Sept. 29, 1796. Alexander Trent, Daniel Grogan, William Grogan.

Book E, page 77. Asa Cummings to Edward Woolen for 38 pds 76 A on br of Wolf Island Cr adj sd Cummings & Wollen, Richard Coram. May 26, 1796. A. Philips, Thomas Lowe.

Book E, page 78. William Kellam to Spencer Kellam for a valuable sum 100 A on William Kellams Mill br. Dec. 26, 1796. Thomas Jamison, William Motley, William Kallam.

Book E, page 79. William Sillivan to John Pearson for 100 pds 100 A on Hogans Cr. July 20, 1796. Thomas Lowe, John Edmundson, Danl Lowe.

Book E, page 80. Aron Allen & William Jones to William Oliver for 30 pds 300 A on Troublesome & Jacobs Crs adj George Brown, William Pratt, Alexander Brown, Moses Short, Thomas Lomacks. Mar. 28, 1795. Nathl. Linder, Vincent Wheeler.

Book E, page 81. Joseph Tharp of Rowan Co. to Sampson Lanier for

50 pds 200 A on Little Hogans Cr adj Thomas Bowen. Nov. 24, 1796. A. Philips, Stephen Neal.

Book E, page 82. Hugh Lynch to Jacob Young for 13 pds 14 sh 67 A on Haw R adj Richard Rossell, Mary Patrick, William Buckanon, being land bought from John Stanford. June 20, 1796. James Mateer, John Lynch.

Book E, page 83. William Bethell to Thomas Sparks Jr. for 50 pds 108 A on Hogans Cr adj William McCollum. Feb. 22, 1797. Jno Hunter, Rich Bethell.

Book E, page 84. Philip Anglen of Henry Co., Va. to Benjamin Smith for 50 pds 55 A on Mayo R adj sd Smith. Mar. 18, 1796. Zachariah King, Field Trent, Alex. Trent, Jesse Odell.

Book E, page 85. Asa Cummings to Henry Kilmon for 75 pds 30 A adj sd Kilmon, Woolen. Feb. 28, 1797. John Abbot.

Book E, page 86. Joshua Smith to James Sharp for 40 pds 100 A on Mayo R adj sd Sharp, Thomas Joyce, James Scales. May 23, 1796. Samuel Shelton, Isham Sharp.

Book E, page 87. Sharp Hamilton of S.C. to Samuel Fielder for 20 pds pd to George Hamilton 200 A adj Caswell Co. line, Harrison Watkins, Harris, Adams, being grant of George Hamilton dec'd of which Sharp Hamilton is Heir at law. Oct. 25, 1796. John Starrat, William Walker, John W. Jones.

Book E, page 88. John McElroy & wife Ann to Ebenezer Patrick for 50 pds 100 A on Haw R adj Mary Patrick, James S. McElroy. Mar. 1, 1796. William Patrick, Mathew Covey.

Book E, page 89. Nathan Okey to John Lemon Jr. for 20 pds 100 A on Buffalo Cr, Stokes Co. line. Feb. 4, 1797. Robt Strong, John Strong, John Lemon Sr.

Book E, page 90. Job Baker to John Young Sr. for 60 pds 100 A on Rockhouse Cr adj Joseph Cunningham, Aron Allen, James Brown. Jan. 14, 1797. A. Philips, R. Boak, J. Pursell.

Book E, page 91. Stephen Lephew to David Hyler for 30 pds 100 A on Whetstone Cr adj George Peay. Aug. 12, 1796. David Scales, Nicholas Overby, Philip Maberry.

Book E, page 92. Christopher Vandergriff of Lancaster Co., S.C. to Benjamin Webb for 400 pds 247 A on Dan R & Gr Troublesome Cr adj Lovelatty. Feb. 25, 1797. William Jones, Thomas Coalsion, John Wafford.

Book E, page 93. William Walker to William Sutherland for 40 pds 100 A on Cirbys Cr of Dan R. Dec. 1, 1795. John Morgan, James Walker.

Book E, page 94. State of N.C. to Joseph Odell 100 A on Mayo R. Dec. 20, 1796.

Book E, page 95. State of N.C. to Joseph Odell 50 A. Dec.20,1796.

Book E, page 96. State of N.C. to Peter Oliver 100 A adj John Oliver, James Oliver, Thomas Henderson. Dec. 20, 1796.

Book E, page 97. Charles Shickle to Jacob Bean for 50 pds 25½ A on Pruets fork of Hogans Cr adj David Settle. 1795. Walter Hedrick, Charles Been, Samuel Watt.

Book E, page 98. John Challes to Charles Skinner for 50 pds 60 A adj Caswell Co. line. Jan. 20, 1797. Thomas Duncan, Thomas Cox, Benjamin Hardister.

Book E, page 99. John Challes to Thomas Cox of Caswell Co. for 15 pds 12 sh Va. money 22 A on Greens Cr adj Caswell Co. line. Jan. 27, 1797. Thomas Duncan, Benjamin Hardister, Thomas Skinner.

Book E, page 100. George Ward of Pitsilvania Co., Va. to Leven Downs for 50 pds Va. money 100 A on Wolf Island Cr adj Mathew Mills, London, Larrimore, Brown. Feb. 25, 1793. George Adams, Andrew J. Lynch, Robert Astin, Samuel French.

Book E, page 101. Sampson Lanier to James Reagon for 200 pds 300 A on Upper Hogans Cr adj William Flemming, Warren Walker, John Atkinson, Margery Feagon, William Flamon. Nov. 23, 1795. John Curry, Patrick Twomey.

Book E, page 102. Burwell Peeples to Thomas Perkins of Pitsylvania Co., Va. for 171 pds 228 A on Haw R adj James Patrick, Jonas Frost, Hubbard Peeples. Aug. 31, 1795. Abraham Peeples, Hubbard Peeple.

Book E, page 103. William Cockrill to John Watt for 100 pds 216 A on Pruets Cr. Nov. 24, 1794. Lewis Cockrill, Levy Garrison. (Frances Cockrill signs with William Cockrill.)

Book E, page 104. Thomas Guttery to William Denny for 80 pds 250 A on Hogans Cr adj John Holms, Sillivant Pierson. Sept. 5, 1796. John Starrat, James Walker, Peter Marcilliot.

Book E, page 105. Robert Galloway to Zachariah Wall of Culpepper Co., Va. for 200 pds Va. money 187 A on N side Dan R adj Joseph Scales, Mrs. Overton, being land seized from Batte C. Lacy who relinquished title. Apr. 27, 1797. John Menzies, Epaphrodites White, Turbyfield Barns, Thomas Jamison.

Book E, page 106. John Harper & wife Margaret to William Granger & Benjamin Granger for certain sum her third of land from the estate of her dec'd husband, Benjamin Granger. Feb. 20, 1797. Walter Martin, Samuel Herrin.

Book E, page 107. James McCaleb of Wilks Co. to Ezekiel Wheeler for 200 pds 200 A on Little Troublesome Cr. May 15, 1797. John Hallum, Vincent Wheeler.

Book E, page 108. John Warner to Robert Cummings for 50 pds 150 A on Haw R being grant in 1782 to sd Warner. July 5, 1794. Isaac Perriman, Samuel Rhodes.

Book E, page 109. James Campbell to Sampson Lanier for 50 pds 24½ A on Big Troublesome Cr adj James Whitesells. Mar. 15, 1797. A. Philips, Moses McClean.

Book E, page 110. David Bernard of Davidson Co., Tenn. to John Sims for 20 pds 50 A on Still House Cr of Dan R adj sd Bernard, Thomas Henderson. May 26, 1797.

Book E, page 111. Elmore Walker to Elisha Wade of Charlotte Co., Va. for 3 pds 8 A on Moses Cr adj sd Walker, Thomas Henderson, Widow Scurry. Feb. 23, 1797. Robt. Napier, Thos. Lowe.

Book E, page 112. Sutton McCollister to John Pound for 40 pds 75 A on Gr Rockhouse Cr adj Allen Williams, Perkle. Oct. 28, 1796. John Linder, Severigan Butt.

Book E, page 113. John Leak Esq to John Peay for $10.00 ½ A lot in town of Leaksville. May 1, 1796. Zach. Strong, Thos. Peay, William Cayton.

Book E, page 114. Mary Fields to Elisha Joyce for 16 pds 111 A on Sharps Cr & on Mayo Mountain adj John Pratt, William Lybass, Joshua Smith. Jan. 19, 1795. Jarrat Patterson, Allen Fields.

Book E, page 115. John Witty of Guilford Co. to Ezekiel Witty for 30 pds 68 A on N side Haw R adj James Delay, Andrew Witty. Jan. 26, 1797. A. Philips, Joseph Bennet, Andrew Witty.

Book E, page 116. Joseph Still & wife Elizabeth and Mary Warner to Robert Cummings for 75 pds 150 A on Haw R adj sd Cummings, Malaki Reives, Thomas Moore (formerly William Reves). Oct. 14, 1790. Joseph Wheetley, Rowlen Williams, Joseph Rhodes.

Book E, page 117. Alexander Joyce Esq, High Sheriff to John Peay for 25 pds 200 A adj Sampson Lanier, John Howell, Benjamin Stone, Ezekiel Kory, Dill, being land seized by order of court & sold to highest bidder to satisfy debt of Thomas Howell as recovered by Asa Brasher of Guilford Co. May 23, 1797. Tho. Henderson, Jno. C. Cox.

Book E, page 118. Benjamin Spencer, John Spencer & Thomas Spencer to Robert Donaldson, merchant of Fayetteville, for 1500 pds 180 A on Haw R including Water grist mill, oil mill & Distillary. Sept. 12, 1794. William Herbin, John Harbin, James Thornburn.

Book E, page 119. Benjamin Spencer to Robert Donaldson, merchant of Fayetteville for 5 pds 12 A on Haw R. 1794. William Harbin, John Spencer, James Thornburn.

Book E, page 120. Thomas Lomax to Moses Lomax for 50 pds & for love and affection for his son 200 A on Troublesome Cr adj Elijah Wittie, John Cummings. May 23, 1797. A. Philips, V. Wheeler.

Book E, page 121. John Leak Esq to John Peay for $25.00 2 lots in Town of Leaksville. May 31, 1796. Zach Strong, Thos. Peay, Wm. Cayton.

Book E, page 122. Benjamin Smith to Lurania Smith for 50 pds 55 A on N side Mayo R adj sd Smith, Alexander Trent. May 23, 1796. Daniel Grogan, John Grogan, William Grogan.

Book E, page 123. Robert Martin to David McCollum for 40 pds 277 A on NE fork of Jacobs Cr adj James Walker, John Wilson. Mar. 5, 1796. Samuel Trolinger.

Book E, page 124.   John Hampton of Henry Co., Va. to Namon Ro-
berts for 100 pds 120 A on Whetstone Cr adj John Lemon, Sneed
Strong.   Feb. 4, 1797.   T. Garland, Archebald Murphey, Joseph
Hoper.

Book E, page 125.   John Leak Esq to William Cayten for $10.00
½ A lot in Town of Leaksville on Henry Street.   July 13, 1796.
Thos. Peay, Alex. Sneed, Robert Coleman.

Book E, page 126.   Charles Baker to John Owen for 150 pds 325 A
being three tracts on Piney Cr.   Mar. 11, 1797.   John Pound,
David Owen.

Book E, page 127.   William Martin to Joel Foster for 20 pds 200
A on Mayo R and Bever Island Cr adj Joel Mackey.   Dec. 5, 1796.
Joshua Smith, William Gill, John Amos Jr.

Book E, page 128.   Peter Scales of Patrick Co., Va. to William
Holt for 75 pds 150 A on W side Mayo R near top of Mayo Mountain
adj Joshua Smith, Andrew Joyce.   May 15, 1797.   Joel Foster, Bud
Holt, Agga Amos.

Book E, page 129.   William Jones to James Maxwell for 375 pds
500 A on Troublesome Cr adj Robert Barr, Hugh Linch.   Oct. 13,
1796.   Walter Marr, Aaron Lord, Walker Thomas.

Book E, page 130.   John Conner to Richard Simpson for 36 pds 121
A on Jacobs Cr adj Alexander Martin Esq, Charles Bruce, Samuel
Short, William Conner.   Mar. 24, 1796.   Robert Napier Jr.,
Thomas Simpson.

Book E, page 131.   John Mathews to Bird Deatherage for 300 cur-
rent money 150 A on W side Mayo R adj sd Deatherage, Elijah
Joyce, Andrew Joyce, William Jennings.   Jan. 23, 1797.   William
Jennings, Robert Joyce.

Book E, page 132.   Edmund Haggard of Clark Co., Ky. to John
Wheeler Jones for 200 pds 200 A on Mill Cr adj Harris, George
Adams, William Williams, William Robison.   Apr. 17, 1795.   Hans.
Humphrey, Martin Wisiner.

Book E, page 133.   Elmore Walker to Elisha Wade of Charlotte Co.,
Va. for 50 pds 92 A on Moses Cr adj Thomas Henderson.   Feb. 23,
1797.   Thomas Lowe, Robt. Napier.

Book E, page 134.   Isham Simmons to James Daniel for 100 pds 100
A on Piney Fork adj Brochus.   Nov. 25, 1797.   John Simmons,
Robert Lilley.

Book E, page 135.   Margret Dimond to Jeremiah Pritchet for 80
pds 227 A on Little Troublesome Cr.   May 25, 1797.   John Hallum,
Vin. Wheeler.

Book E, page 136.   Daniel Allen to Benjamin Allen for 50 pds 127
A on Hogans Cr adj Nathaniel Williams, Daniel Allen Sr.   179_.

Book E, page 137.   John McCubbin & wife Sopha to John Bloyd for
100 pds 100 A adj Mark London.   Sept. 18, 1792.   William McCollum,
John Odell, Jonathan Griffith.

Book E, page 138.   State of N.C. to John Oliver 60 A on Dan R
adj Robert Gilleland, Isaac Whitworth.   Feb. 22, 1797.

Book E, page 139. State of N.C. to Alem B. Williams 100 A on both sides Town Cr adj Thomas Raferty. June 27, 1793.

Book E, page 140. State of N.C. to Robert Joyce 80 A on Mayo R adj Philip Deatherage. July 16, 1795.

Book E, page 141. Hanah Waybon to William Bethell for 20 pds 20 A on Pruets fork of Hogans Cr, being part of old survey of Thompson Harris and one third of land deeded to Waybon Heirs. 1795. Charles Mitchell, Daniel Parker, Rich. Bethell.

Book E, page 142. Daniel Parker to William Bethell for 50 pds 20 A on Hogans Cr adj John Horsford, John Watts, Samuel Watts, being tract deed to Heirs of William Waybon by Thompson Harris & Robert Harris, land becoming mine after intermarriage with heir of William Waybon. Apr. 15, 1795. William Tranum, Richd. Bethell, Charles Mitchel.

Book E, page 143. Edward Philpott of Henry Co., Va. to William Bethell for 50 pds 86 A on Hogans Cr. Mar. 4, 1797. John Thrasher, R. Bethell, Robert Mullin.

Book E, page 144. James McCallum to William Bethell for 100 pds 170 A on Hogans Cr adj Joseph McClain, line of Daniel McCollum dec'd. Apr. 8, 1795. Robert Kimbrough, Rich. Bethell.

Book E, page 145. George Norman & wife Caroline, formerly widow of Abraham Spencer to William Bethell for 10 pds 100 A, being my thirds of a tract of land Abraham Spencer lived and died on. Aug. 1, 1797. Sherwood Toney, Charles Mitchell, R. Bethell.

Book E, page 146. James McCubbin to John Morehead of Pitsylvania Co., Va. for 43 3/4 A on Burchfields fork of Wolf Island Cr adj Peter Martin, William Patterson, Francis Patterson, being part of grant to John Simmons, then sold to sd McCubbin. July 18, 1797. Sherwood Toney, Dudley Jones, James McCullough, Ezekiel Murphy.

Book E, page 147. Shiveral Garner to Edward Newnam for 50 pds 60 A on Little Troublesome Cr adj sd Newnam, William Spiers, Road leading from Dixie Ferry to Iron Works. Nov. 6, 1795. John Harper, Salathiel Newnam.

Book E, page 148. Martin Wisenor to John Pennix of Caswell Co. for 75 pds Va. money 125 A on N side Haw R adj John Wheeler Jones. Oct. 13, 1796. Andrew Wilson, John Pritchet.

Book E, page 149. John Pennix of Caswell Co. to John Brown for 80 pds Va. money 125 A adj John W. Jones. Dec. 4, 1796. Wm. Brown, James Brown.

Book E, page 150. Henry Wisenor to James Smith for 150 pds 184 A on High Rock Cr of Haw R adj John W. Jones, John Brown. Aug. 14, 1797. William Walker, John W. Jones.

Book E, page 151. David Poyner & wife Joanna of Caswell Co. to Edward Nunon for 50 pds 50 A on Little Troublesome Cr adj sd Newnam, Peter Perkins. Nov. 3, 1795. John Harper, Thomas Poyner.

Book E, page 152. John Stanford to William Hancock for 40 pds

100 A on Troublesome Cr adj William Buckanon.   Nov. 18, 1795.   A.
Philips, William Atkison.

Book E, page 153.   Selethem Tewnam to John Harper for 45 pds 100
A on Little Troublesome Cr adj Abraham Philips, Edward Newnam.
Nov. 6, 1795.   Edward Newnam, Shiveral Garner.

Book E, page 154.   Joseph Still to Joseph Wheatly of Guilford Co.
for 50 pds 50 A on brs of Haw R adj John Thadesis.   Jan. 28,
1795.   John Rhodes, Samuel Rhodes.

Book E, page 155.   John Horsford & wife Elizabeth to Moses Garri-
son for 100 pds 290 A on Pruets fork of Hogans Cr adj Thomas
Sparks, Thomas Mullin, William Mount, Hays, William Bethell,
McClain.   Jan. 20, 1796.

Book E, page 156.   John Spencer to Charles Payne for 100 pds 96
A on Haw R adj John Cunningham.   Jan. 20, 1796.   James Smith,
Jesse Payne.

Book E, page 157.   Jeremiah Thacker & wife Mary Ann to Benjamin
Moore for 50 pds 100 A on Hogans Cr adj Samuel Watt.   Oct. 4,
1796.   John Matlock, Isaiah Hancock, James Bateman.

Book E, page 158.   James Rigsby to Joseph Still for 50 pds 50 A
on N side Haw R adj Rhodes.   Dec. 17, 1794.   John Rhodes, Samuel
Rhodes.

Book E, page 159.   John Stanford to William Atkison for 52 pds
105 A on N side Haw R adj William Buchanon.   Nov. 18, 1795.   A.
Philips, Samuel McSparran.

Book E, page 160.   Edward Woolen to Asa Cummins for 10 pds 30 A
on Wolf Island Cr adj sd Cummings, Henry Kilman.   Aug. 31, 1797.
John Pound, A. Philips.

Book E, page 161.   James London to James Taylor for 50 pds 96 A
on Lickfork adj sd Taylor, John Harris, Isaiah Hancock, Henry
Sanders.   Nov. 1795.   Baily Martin, John Harris, Horford Taylor.

Book E, page 162.   Thomas Lomax to William Lomax Jr. for 100 pds
& for the better maintainance of his son William Lomax 229 A on
both sides Big Troublesome Cr adj Moses Lomax, George Brown,
Samuel Maxwell, Elijah Witty.   June 13, 1797.   A. Philips, James
Martin.

Book E, page 163.   May 29, 1797.   Gift Deed of Hubbard Peeples
of Guilford Co. for love and affection for Edward Robinson Peeples
250 A on Gr Troublesome Cr adj Richard Lovetts.   Thomas Perkins,
A. Peeples.

Book E, page 164.   John Curry & wife Sarah Curry to William Jones
Sr. for 520 silver dollars 175 A on N side Haw R adj John Mateer,
Moses Curry, Robert Curry, being land laid out unto John Curry
Jr. from estate of John Curry Sr. dec'd.   July 13, 1797.   A.
Boyd, John Jones, Thomas Jones.

Book E, page 165.   Adam Trolinger to Peter Simpson for 60 pds
106 A on rocky fork of Jacobs Cr adj Nathaniel Linder, John
Stockard, Alex. Martin Esq.   Aug. 13, 1796.   Saml. Trolinger, Wm
Cunningham.

Book E, page 166. State of N.C. to James Jackson 400 A on Hickory Cr of Mayo R adj Abraham Martin, Champ Gibson. Oct.29,1783.

Book E, page 167. State of N.C. to William Mills 18 A on E side Mayo R and Green Springs Br adj Joshua Mabery, William Kellam, Joel Gibson. Nov. 17, 1790.

Book E, page 168. William Caldwell to Samuel Watt for 100 pds 120 A on Hogans Cr adj Willis Pruet. Mar. 8, 1795. Wm. McCallum, John Matlock.

Book E, page 169. William Winstead & wife Betsy to Henry Scales for 100 pds 200 A on S side Buffalo Cr adj sd Scales, John Strong, John Lemon. Aug. 31, 1797. W. Bethell, Rich. Bethell.

Book E, page 170. James Daniel to Samuel Bollock for 100 pds 100 A on Piney Fork adj Brockas. Feb. 17, 1797. Robt Lilley, Augustine Browder.

Book E, page 171. Isaac Perryman & wife Margaret to Alexander Martin Esq for 12 pds 17 A adj sd Perryman & Martin. Sept. 17, 1796. John Thomas, Ro. Martin.

Book E, page 172. Jeremiah Poston and Cornelus Davis of Caswell Co. to Thomas Sertain for sum 120 A on Hogans Cr. Oct. 20, 1794. John Dilworth, Thomas Key, Alexander Paschal(?), Joe Scott.

Book E, page 173. John Stanford to Asa Hollowell for 221 pds 6 sh 8 p 332 A on Haw R adj Michael Caffy, Wafford, William Adkison, Widow Buchanon, Nathan Guerin, Samuel Moore. Mar. 4, 1796. Emanuel ? James, Stephen Stacy.

Book E, page 174. Robert Curry to John Cryer for 100 pds 56 A on Big Troublesome Cr & Haw R adj William Boyd, John Curry, Jno. Holms. Aug. 22, 1797. William Jones, Thomas Thompson, Thomas Coolscott.

Book E, page 175. Robert Curry to John Cryer for 50 pds 4 A on N side Haw R adj John Curry. Aug. 22, 1797. William Jones, Thomas Thompson, Thos. Coolscott.

Book E, page 176. Robert Curry to John Cryer for 140 pds 97 A on Haw R. Aug. 22, 1797. William Jones, Thos. Thompson, Thos. Coolscott.

Book E, page 177. Robert Curry to John Cryer for 200 pds 250 A on Schoolhouse Br of Haw R. Aug. 22, 1797. William Jones, Thomas Thompson, Thos. Coolscott.

Book E, page 178. Allen Williams to John Pound for 60 pds 100 A on Big Rockhouse Cr adj Sutton McCollister, Nehemiah King, Robert Galloway, Thos. Larkin, Thos. King. Sept. 2, 1797. Luke Bernard, John Fields.

Book E, page 179. Joshua Smith Esq, High Sheriff to Andrew Ector for 10 pds 1 sh 50 A, being seized by court order to satisfy debt of Moses Dean as recovered by William Jones. Aug. 30, 1797. R. Galloway, A. Boyd.

Book E, page 180. William Hill to William Mills for 100 pds 382 A on Buffalo Island Cr adj Joseph Gibson, Gustavis Hill. Mar. 10, 1788. Chas. Galloway, A. Walker, Leo Murray.

Book E, page 181. Isaac Clark, former Sheriff to Sherwood Toney for 11 pds 1 sh 200 A on Wolf Island Cr adj William Tranom, Elizabeth Bruce. Aug. 13, 1797. Charles Mitchell, Richard Bethell.

Book E, page 182. State of N.C. to Joseph Cunningham 50 A on Jacobs Cr adj sd Cunningham, Sutton McCollister. July 16,1795.

Book E, page 183. John Dill Sr. & wife Mary to William McCallum for 150 pds 153 A on Wolf Island Cr adj Samuel Watt. Aug. 24, 1797. William Bethell, John Challes.

Book E, page 184. Gift Deed of Raf (Ralph) Leftrage Norris to granddaus Salley Sharp, Elizabeth Sharp and Rachel Sharp all my goods & chattels now being in my present dwelling house. Apr. 10, 1797. Ben Hamlen, John Brim.

Book E, page 185. Sharp Hamilton of Guilford Co. to William & John Herbin for 150 pds 300 A on Haw R, being part of tract sd Hamilton inherited as Heir at law of George Hamilton dec'd. Aug. 28, 1797. Hanson Humphrys, George Herbin.

Book E, page 186. Laurance Porter & wife Mary Ann to Rachel Russell for 70 pds 440 A on Wolf Island & Quaqua Cr adj Christo-pher Dudley. Sept. 25, 1797. Coloson Porter, Ransom Dudley, Mathew Smith, John Smith.

Book E, apge 187. David Hyler to Thomas Peay for 60 pds 100 A adj George Peay, John Bellanfant, Stephen Lephew. Nov. 1797. William T. Morton, George Peay Jr.

Book E, page 188. James Taylor to John Horford Taylor for 45 pds 96 A on Lickfork adj John Harris, Isaiah Hancock, Henry Saunders. Nov. 7, 1797. Jesse Kerr, William Saunders.

Book E, page 189. John Davis to William McCallum for 10 pds 30 A on Lickfork Cr adj Thomas Sparks. Nov. 25, 1797. Will. Be-thell, John Challes.

Book E, page 190. William Thorp of Iredel Co. to William Fields for 100 pds 162½ A on S side Troublesome Cr adj Guilford Co. line. July 26, 1796. Burges Stone, Epraim Thompson.

Book E, page 191. John Lacy & William Lacy to Henry Baughan for 103 pds 10 sh Va. money 131 A on S side Dan R adj Edward Reynols, Samuel Garner. Nov. 24, 1797. Robert Wall, Edward Reynols, A. B. Walker, Vall Allen.

Book E, page 192. John & William Lacy to Edward Reynolds for 103 pds 103 A on S side Dan R adj Henry Baughan, Fare. Nov. 24, 1797. Robert Wall, A. B. Walker, Vall Allen, Henry Baughan.

Book E, page 193. Jacob Cantrill to Absalom Goostree for $100 150 A on Wolf Island Cr adj Elijah Cantrell, Luke Barnard, John Granger. Sept. 23, 1797. Tho. Pound, John Harrison, John Abbet.

Book E, page 194. Robert Means to William Means for (no price mentioned) 200 A on Mayo R adj Humphry Brooks. Nov. 28, 1797.

Peter Hunter, James Riddle, Elizabeth Means.

Book E, page 195. Nehemiah Vernon to Jonathan Vernon for 40 pds 131 A on Mayo R adj Samuel Dalton. Nov. 28, 1797. John Vernon, Sarah Sims Vernon, Jane Caldwell Vernon.

Book E, page 196. Ralph Norris to Joseph Roberts for 20 pds 150 A on Rocky Br being a grant from State to sd Norris. Oct. 17, 1797. John Reagon, Samuel Brown, Rachel Roberts.

Book E, page 197. Peter Williams to John Challes for 42 pds 16 sh 3 p 34½ A on Wolf Island Cr adj Abner Parrot, John Milbey. Jan. 20, 1797. Abner Parrott, Isaac Hill.

Book E, page 198. James Galloway to William Thornton Morton for 250 pds 400 A on Whetstone Cr adj George Peay, being a grant in 1779 to Giles Carter later sold to sd Galloway. Oct. 25, 1797. T. Garland, James Taylor.

Book E, page 199. John Jones to Robert Wall for 150 pds Va. money 400 A on Reed Cr adj Col. James Martin. Nov. 3, 1797. Joshua Smith, Abner Walker, Zachariah Wall.

Book E, page 200. Hezekiah Corry to John Heath for 35 pds 80 A on Big Troublesome Cr & crossing Kings Br adj sd Heath & Corry. Jan. 24, 1797. A. Philips, John Flemin.

Book E, page 201. Samuel Purnal in Right of his wife Elizabeth as an heir of the estate of Thomas George Richard Turner dec'd together with the other heirs George Sears Turner, Hester Turner, Martha Turner, Margaret Turner, Mary Turner to James Maxwell for 50 pds 103 A on Big Troublesome Cr, being the tract Samuel Purnal now lives on adj William Buckanon. Sept. 20, 1797. Thomas Covey, Mary Holt, William Mooney. (Also signing was William Cartwright in right of his wife.)

Book E, page 202. Turbafield Barnes to Nathaniel Scales 1000 pds 335½ A on E side Mayo R & on the top and S side Mayo Mountain and on road leading to Mountain Meeting House into road from Moravian Town to Petersburg, adj Robert Axton, Richard Vernon, James Harrison, Robert Warren, Thos. Pratt. Apr. 27, 1797. John Leak, Philip Ross.

Book E, page 203. Joshua Smith, High Sheriff to Thomas Barnard for 33 pds 180 A on Little Rockhouse Cr being land seized by order of court to satisfy debt of John Hunter dec'd as recovered by John Morton. Mar. 11, 1797. John Fields, Newsam Barham.

Book E, page 204. Robertson Ross to Reubin Ross for 50 pds 75 A on Little Rockhouse Cr. Feb. 26, 1797. Leaven Mitchell, Solomon Mitchell.

Book E, page 205. John McCarrol to John Mackey for 30 pds 60 A on Piney Br adj sd Mackey, John Pirkle. Sept. 15, 1797. J. McCarroll, Guy Vermillion.

Book E, page 206. Alexander Lyall of Stokes Co. and George Hunter to Humphry Brooks for a valuable sum 160 A on both sides Mayo R adj Robert Means, Peter Hunter, William Motley. Jan. 16, 1796. Peter Hunter, Spencer Kellum, William Motley, Richard Martin.

Book E, page 207. William Moore & wife Elizabeth of Henry Co., Va. to Chesly Barnes for 90 pds 250 A on both sides Buffalo Cr adj Stokes Co. line. Nov. 22, 1793. Robert Means, William Kellum, Wm. Motley.

Book E, page 208. Ann Booker Overton & Batte C. Lacy & wife Elizabeth to Richard Wall for 300 pds Va. money 338 A on Beaver Island Cr on N side Dan R adj John Watson, John Davis, Thomas Joyce, Edmund Brewer (lately George Judge), Theophilus Lacy. Nov. 27, 1797. James Scales, Thomas Sims, Zachariah Wall.

Book E, page 209. Thomas Crawley of Stokes Co. to Jesse Gowen (Goin) for 50 pds land on Daltons & Hickory Crs and Stokes Co. line. Oct. 27, 1797. John Amos Sr., Daniel Cardwell, Rich. Wheeler.

Book E, page 210. Thomas Crawley of Stokes Co. to John Ridley for 25 pds 75 A on Daltons & Hickory Cr & Stokes Co. line. Oct. 27, 1797. John Amos Sr., Daniel Cardwell, Richard Wheeler.

Book E, page 211. Nathan Cardwell to William Blake for 50 pds 200 A on Daltons Cr adj Champ Gibson, James Jackson, Abram Martin. Sept. 30, 1797. Nicholas Dalton, Peter Hunter.

Book E, page 212. Thomas Asher to Charles Moore for 20 pds 50 A on Beaver Island Cr adj Anthony Dearing, Henderson, Stokes Co. line. Oct. 17, 1796. J. B. Pittman, John Vawter, Saml. Henderson.

Book E, page 213. William Stratton to William Webster for 100 pds 208 A being land on which sd Webster now lives adj Duncan Beath. Nov. 22, 1797. Charles Moore, William Nickel.

Book E, page 214. State of N.C. to James Martin 395 A on Mill Cr commonly called Hogans Cr adj sd Martin, John Reagon, Philip Gates. Warrant dated Aug. 15, 1779. Nov. 25, 1797.

Book E, page 215. State of N.C. to Pleasant Henderson Assignee of Robert Martin 150 A on Jacobs Cr adj sd Henderson, James Hays. Nov. 25, 1797.

Book E, page 216. State of N.C. to Isaac Dolton 30 A on E side Mayo R adj sd Dalton. July 9, 1794.

Book E, page 217. James Frost & wife Isabel to William Case for $240 192 A on Big Troublesome Cr adj Richard Rossell, line of John Marr dec'd. May 23, 1798. Jonas Frost Jr.

Book E, page 218. Thomas Perkins to Hubbard Peeples of Guilford Co. for 5 sh 50 A on S side Haw R adj tract where sd Perkins lives, James Patrick. May 27, 1798. Joseph T. Joyce, Martha Joyce.

Book E, page 219. Hubbard Peeples of Guilford Co. to Thomas Perkins for 5 sh 50 A on N side Haw R adj tract on which sd Peeples lives, Joseph T. Joyce. May 27, 1798. Jos. T. Joyce, Martha Joyce.

Book E, page 220. Moses Barrow of Stokes Co. to Hugh McKillip of Stokes Co. for 200 pds 250 A on Kerbys Cr. Mar. 31, 1798. Andrew McKillip, John McDowell, James Burnes.

Book E, page 221. William Harris to William Carrico for 50 pds 100 A on Hogans Cr adj Moore, Wheeler, Hodge. Mar. 4, 1797. V. Wheeler.

Book E, page 222. John McKenny to James Roach for 80 pds Va. money land on Little Rockhouse Cr adj Mary Elliott. Sept. 4, 1797. James Fitzgerald.

Book E, page 223. John George to Charles Moore for 24 pds 45 A on Big Troublesome Cr adj sd Moore & George, Robert Barr. Dec. 27, 1797. George Leoman, Robert Barr.

Book E, page 224. John Joyce & wife Nancy to Elijah Joyce for 160 pds Va. money 441 A on Shepherds Cr. Dec. 25, 1792. Joel Bondurant, Drury Bondurant, Levi Davis, William Sharp, Robert Joyce.

Book E, page 225. Elijah Joyce to John Joyce (coon) for 300 pds 222½ A on Shepherds Cr adj sd Elijah Joyce, Bird Deatherage, Richard Vernon, William Jennings. May 31, 1798. Vall Allen, Robert Joyce.

Book E, page 226. Allen Williams to Thomas Pound for $15, 11 A on Wolf Island Cr. May 30, 1798. Daniel Allen, Jno. Pound.

Book E, page 227. John Leak Esq to Thomas Carr of Henry Co., Va. for $20 ½ A lot in Town of Leaksville on Water Street. May 29, 1798. Terry Hughes, T. Garland.

Book E, page 228. John Leak to John Reynolds for $10 ½ A lot in Town of Leaksville on Patrick Street, being No. 21 in Plat. Dec. 16, 1797. Terry Hughes, William Cayton.

Book E, page 229. Thomas Nelson to James Lowe for 175 pds all my right title to land on which my father deceased. Sept. 2, 1795. Thos. Lowe, William Nelson.

Book E, page 229. John Fields Esq, Sheriff, to Mary Linder for 31.9.9 124 A on Jacobs Cr as highest bidder on land seized by order of William Bethell C. C. for debt against estate of Nathaniel Linder dec'd as recovered by James Wright, David McCollum, Joshua Skinner. Mar. 2, 1798. R. Galloway, A. Philips.

Book E, page 231. Patrick Mullen to Robert Lomax of Guilford Co. for 50 pds 200 A on Jacobs Cr. Feb. 14, 1796. Moses Lomax, Thomas Lomax, Marget Lomax.

Book E, page 232. David Dalton of Stokes Co. to James Edwards for 200 pds proc money 300 A on N side Mayo R adj Nehemiah Vernon. May 1798. Richard Bostick, Elisha Elexander, Agustin Samuel. (Isaac Dalton signed with David Dalton.)

Book E, page 233. John Leak Esq to Terry Hughes of Henry Co., Va. for $20 ½ A lot in Town of Leaksville on N side Water Street, being No. 20. May 29, 1798. John Gibson, T. Garland.

Book E, page 234. John Matlock Esq, Sheriff, to Jesse Dillon of Guilford Co. for 14 pds 200 A adj John Holloway, Samuel Young, Widow Bowen, being land seized for debt of Morris Lewis. May 28, 1798. W. Bethell.

Book E, page 234. Alexander Joyce, High Sheriff, to Thomas Grogan for 20 pds 200 A on Lickfork of Buffalo Island Cr adj Joseph Gibson, being land seized by order of court for debt of James Pratt as recovered by John Wilson & son Peter. May 23, 1797. Richard Bethell, Thomas Roberts, Lewis Odell, Jno. Peay.

Book E, page 236. Absalom Harvey to Peter Harden for 20 pds 45 A on Country Line Cr adj Thomas Hardin. Henry Harden, George Hornbuckle.

Book E, page 237. John Fields, High Sheriff, to Adam Winders for 20 pds 110 A on Piney Fork of Troublesome Cr adj Joseph Curry, being land seized by order of court and advertised and sold to highest bidder for debt of Bartlett Estes. Sept. 1, 1797. Thos. Peay, George Douglas.

Book E, page 238. Robert Wray to William Martin for 16 pds 10 sh 16½ A on Hogans Cr adj Robert Wray, Andrew Wray. Mar. 1, 1798.

Book E, page 239. John Leak to Sarah Davison for 100 pds 200 A on a br of Dan R adj Coleman, John Gibson. May 26, 1798. T. Garland, Motley Owen.

Book E, page 240. William Standard of Caswell Co. for 30 pds Va. money to William Patterson 100 A on Wolf Island Cr. Apr. 2, 1796. W. McCollum, James Akin, John Odineal.

Book E, page 241. James Hays to James Hayley for 37 pds 10 sh 150 A on Jacobs Cr adj Robert Rolston, Isaac Rolston. Mar. 6, 1798. John Hays, Wm. Pratt.

Book E, page 242. Richard Simpson to Daniel Goff for 15 pds 50 A on Jacobs Cr adj William Conner. Oct. 4, 1797. Wm. Conner, David Simpson.

Book E, page 243. Charles Bruce of Guilford Co. to John Fleming for 25 pds 71 A on Troublesome Cr adj Upton Williamson, John Heath. May 28, 1798. John Heath, Hezekiah Cory.

Book E, page 244. David Dalton of Stokes Co. to Elisha Alexander for 100 pds 200 A on Paw Paw Cr adj James Edwards, Drury Smith, Nehemiah Vernon. May 22, 1798. Jno. Bostick, James Edwards, Augustin Samuel.

Book E, page 245. Henry Kilmon to Elisha Cantrill for $200 212 A on Wolf Island Cr adj sd Cantrell, Edward Woolen, Isaac Cantrell. June 1, 1798. A. Philips.

Book E, page 246. William Hay of Henry Co., Va. to Thomas Smith for 10 sh 2 A on Va. line adj William Kellam. Feb. 17, 1798. John Fields, Drury Smith.

Book E, page 247. Elisha Alexander to Francis Smith for 11 pds 20 A on Paw Paw Cr adj sd Alexander, James Galloway, Drury Smith. May 30, 1798. John Grogan, James Edwards, Bartholomew Grogan.

Book E, page 248. Sarah Kirkpatrick to Mathew Young & Jesse Young for 49 pds 150 A on Hogans Cr. Oct. 19, 1797. John McPeak, Jehu McMin.

Book E, page 249. John Gibson to Joseph Gibson for 55 pds 125 A on Buffalo Island Cr adj Christopher Hand, sd Joseph Gibson. Sept. 10, 1797. Absalom Gibson, Christopher Hand.

Book E, page 250. James Campbell to Samuel Maxwell Sr. of Guilford Co. for 25 pds 10 sh 70 A on br of Haw R adj James Whitesett, Maj Blair. Nov. 27, 1795. Samuel Maxwell, Alex. Maxwell.

Book E, page 251. James Linkey McAbroy to John Robbins for 260 pds 202 A on S side Haw R adj Mary Patrick. Feb. 6, 1797. John Brown, Asa Hollowell.

Book E, page 252. Elijah Cantrell to Henry Kolmon for $150 A on Wolf Island Cr adj Alexander Joyce, Joseph Asbridge, Thomas Pound. June 1, 1798. A. Philips.

Book E, page 253. John Charles Hodge of Marlborough Co., S.C. to Abel Carrico for 100 pds 253 A on Hogans Cr, being orig grant to John Hodge dec'd & to James Hodge and through a division by Heirs fell to me, being called Tract No. 3. Feb. 26, 1798. John Haines, Wm. Hodge.

Book E, page 254. Luke Bernard to Elijah Cantrell for 100 pds 151 A on Wolf Island Cr adj Alexander Joyce, John Pound Jr., Joseph Asbridge. Mar. 11, 1796. A. Philips, Thos. Pound, John Regon.

Book E, page 255. Elijah Joyce to Richard Vernon for 200 pds 170 A on Shepherds Cr adj John Joyce, John Joyce Sr. May 31, 1798. Val Allen, Robert Joyce.

Book E, page 256. State of N.C. to James Fitzjarrel 373 A on Buffalo Island Cr adj Henry Scales, James Strong, Daniel Wilson, Darby Calahanm. Oct. 22, 1782. (No fee or Rev. service mentioned.)

Book E, page 258. Bartholomew Grogan & wife Lurenia to Daniel Grogan for 20 pds 50 A on Papa Cr adj sd B. Grogan. May 20, 1796. William Grogan, Ben Smith.

Book E, page 259. Thomas Lewellen Sr. to Thomas Lewellin Jr. for 30 pds Va. money land on Shepherds Cr adj Samuel Gann, James Siers, William Jenings. Dec. 12, 1795. Joshua Smith, John Smith, Samuel Gann.

Book E, page 260. State of N.C. to John Conner 121 A on Jacobs Cr adj Alexander Martin Esqr, Charles Bruce, Samuel Short, Andrew Conner, William Conner. July 16, 1797.

Book E, page 261. State of N.C. to James Grant 84 A on Lickfork of Hogans Cr adj William Russell, William Mullen, Abraham Benton, Richard Marr. July 1, 1797.

Book E, page 262. Elizabeth Roberts, widow of James Roberts dec'd to Robert Williams for 200 pds 170 A on N side Dan R adj Namon Roberts, Rose. Oct. 23, 1797. Wm. T. Morton, Alexander Johnson.

Book E, page 263. State of N.C. to William Odle 25 A on Matrimony Cr adj Darby Calaham, Joshua Hopper. July 16, 1795.

Book E, page 264. State of N.C. to John Walker 103 A on Curbys

Cr adj John Brim, Isaac Whitworth, Widow Stephens.

Book E, page 265. John Haines of Marlborough Co., S.C. to Thomas
Paine for certain sum 50 A on Little Troublesome Cr adj Jonathan
Hains, John Linder. Nov. 30, 1797. William Webster, Jno. Chas.
Hodge.

Book E, page 266. John Haines of Marlborough Co., S.C. to Jonat-
han Haines for certain sum 50 A on Little Troublesome Cr adj
Daniel Haines, John Linder, Elijah Haines. Feb. 20, 1797. Walter
Martin, James Scarbrough.

Book E, page 267. Alexander Hunter of Hancock Co., Ga. to Susannah Morton for $100 my half of two tracts of land & mill left me
by my grandfather, John Hunter dec'd, Aug. 29, 1777 being date
of his will. Oct. 13, 1797. John Morton, James Thweatt.

Book E, page 268. State of N.C. to Leaven Mitchell 409 A on Town
Cr adj sd Mitchell, Thomas Rafferty, John Young. July 16,1795.

Book E, page 269. James Davis of Guilford Co. to Jonathan Hanes
for 26 pds 5 sh 53 A on Gr Troublesome Cr adj Walter Martin,
Robert Boak. Nov. 1, 1796. Hugh Lynch, Robert Martin.

Book E, page 270. Walter Martin to Hugh Lynch for 33 pds 33 A
on Piney Cr adj Robert Martin. Feb. 3, 1798. John Linch, Robert
Linch.

Book E, page 271. William Thomas of Wilks Co., Ga. to Lewis
Thomas for 16 pds 150 A on Tomlins fork of Sharps Cr adj Turbe-
field Barnes. May 4, 1795. James Galloway, John Strong, Chas.
Galloway.

Book E, page 272. Levy Garrison to David Settle for 50 pds 50 A
on Vaughans Cr adj Thomas Williams. Sept. 20, 1796. William
Bradberry, Moses Garrison, John Garrison.

Book E, page 273. Moses Garrison Sr. to David Settle for $15
18 A adj sd Settle. Dec. 1796. Leaven Harris, Jno. Harris.

Book E, page 274. John Young to Francis McBride for 25 pds 240
A on Gr Rockhouse Cr adj Thomas King Jr, Robert Small, line of
James Brown dec'd. Feb. 8, 1796. A. Philips, V. Wheeler.

Book E, page 275. Abraham Philips to Thomas King Jr. for 5 pds
10 sh 5 A on Big Rockhouse Cr adj sd Philips & King. July 24,
1798. George Loaman, Henry Moore.

Book E, page 276. Julius Fare to Sarah Kirkpatrick for 100 pds
250 A on upper Hogans Cr adj Samuel Young. Oct. 5, 1797. Thomas
Henderson, L. Berry Fare.

Book E, page 277. Isaac Whitworth to John Oliver for 83 pds 65
A on S side Dan R adj sd Oliver, Thomas Brent. Jan. 15, 1798.
George Overton, Polley Overton.

Book E, page 278. James Martin of Stokes Co. to Thomas Searcy
for 100 pds 200 A on Cokers Cr of Dan R adj Alexander Martin,
John Nelson. Aug. 26, 1798. A. Cummins, Alex. Martin.

Book E, page 279. Thomas Sparks & wife Elizabeth to Jeremiah Odell for 100 pds 108 A on Lickfork of Hogans Cr adj William McCollum. Aug. 25, 1798.

Book E, page 280. Gift Deed of Elizabeth Roberts to son James D. Roberts a negro man named Harry. May 1798. Tho. Henderson, R. Galloway.

Book E, page 281. Shadrack Yeoman to Stokes Yeoman for $400 52 A on Little Rockhouse Cr adj Thomas Barnard. Feb. 19, 1798. James Fitzjarold, Lamech Price.

Book E, page 282. John Fields to Charles Harrison for 10 pds 110 A. Feb. 26, 1798. Thomas Strong, William Fields.

Book E, page 283. William Blagg to Isaac Perriman for 52 pds 51 A on Jacobs Cr adj sd Perriman. Aug. 10, 1798. Joseph Perriman, John Thomas.

Book E, page 284. Richard Oakley of Henry Co., Va. to George Hairston of Henry Co., Va. for 20 pds 600 A on Matrimony Cr adj Virginia line, Samuel Gates, John Roach, Henry Grogan. Sept. 14, 1798. Thomas Graves.

Book E, page 285. James Hays to Moses Garrison for 10 pds 18 A on Pruets Cr adj sd Hays & sd Garrison. Dec. 30, 1797. George Wilson, Moses Garrison Jr.

Book E, page 286. William Bradberry to Samuel Dick for 50 pds 50 A on Lickfork. Sept. 29, 1797. John Matlock, Newton Wright, Moses Driskill.

Book E, page 287. William Farrar & wife Amadich to John Thomas for 10 pds 22 A on Jacobs Cr, being part of tract purchased by sd Farrar of John Chadwell now dec'd. Feb. 3, 1797. Isaac Whitworth Jr., Joseph Perriman.

Book E, page 288. George Hairston of Henry Co., Va. to Thomas Grogan of sd Co. for 20 pds 250 A on Timbertree Cr adj William Hill, Gustavis Hill, Henry Grogan, Roach. May 25, 1798. Thomas Graves.

Book E, page 289. William Clark & wife Margaret to John Watt for $1,500 310 A on Hogans Cr, being two tracts. July 13, 1798. Joseph Clark, Isaac Clark.

Book E, page 290. Thomas Williams to Thomas Chance for 50 pds 180 A on N fork of Hogans Cr adj David Vaughan. Nov. 17, 1796. Richard Covey, John Williams, Thomas Williams.

Book E, page 291. William Bethell C.C. asks James Parks and Moses Hill Esqrs and Justices of Fairfield Co., S.C. to examine John Williams & Thomas William Jr. as to their knowledge of deed of 180 A by Thomas Williams Sr. to Thomas Chance. Nov. 28, 1797.

Book E, page 291. James Parks & Moses Hill, Justices of Fairfield Co., S.C. send sworn testimony of John Williams that he was present and saw Thomas Williams Sr sign deed of 180 A to Thomas Chance and saw Richard Covey & Thomas Williams subscribe their names as witnesses to sd deed. Jan. 26, 1798.

Book E, page 292. George & Curtis Morris to Nathaniel Scales for 200 pds 200 A on Fishing Cr adj Peter Curtis, Charles Galloway, Abraham Philips. Nov. 4, 1797. J. H. Scales, Patsey Hewlett.

Book E, page 293. William Beaver & wife Abigail of Stokes Co. to Peter Wilson for 237 pds 12 sh Va. money 270 A on Mayo R adj Sharp, Axton. Jan. 31, 1798. H. Hampton, Theop. Lacy, M. Lacy.

Book E, page 294. Edward Philpot of Henry Co., Va. to Jospeh Scott of Caswell Co. for 80 pds 233 A on E side Hogans Cr. Apr. 25, 1797. John Stone, John Scott, John Horsford.

Book E, page 295. John McCarril to Peter Perkins of Pittsylvania Co., Va. for 10 pds 50 A on Wolf Island Cr. Jan. 21, 1796. A. Philips, R. Boak, Gideon Johnson Sr.

Book E, page 296. Mary Patrick to James Patrick for 60 pds 60 A on Haw R adj sd James Patrick, Ebenezer Patrick. 1797. William Patrick.

Book E, page 297. John Granger to Jacob Cantrell for 14 pds 40 A on Wolf Island Cr. Sept. 15, 1790. Elijah Cantrell, Jacob Philips.

Book E, page 298. James Akin to James McCubbin for 50 pds 200 A on Horsepen Cr adj Elisha Simmons. Nov. 27, 1797. John McCubbin, James Cook.

Book E, page 298. (Two pages of same number.) Thomas Faulkner to James Ervin for $85 100 A on Piney Cr adj John King, John Marr, Robert Small. Feb. 27, 1798. A. Philips.

Book E, page 299. Gift Deed of George Haynes of Charlotte Co. to James Haley in consideration of great good will toward sd Haley and his family, 1 negro girl named Betty. Nov. 5, 1797. John Spencer, John Hanes.

Book E, page 299. Henry Coulson to John Joyce for 40 pds 100 A on N side Beaver Island Cr and both sides Rich Bottom Br adj sd Joyce, James Hunter. Dec. 5, 1797. James Hunter, Samuel Hunter.

Book E, page 301. James Patrick to John Wafford for 70 pds 4 A on both sides Kennedys Cr including the old Mill. Dec. 4, 1797.

Book E, page 302. Charles Cantrill to Elijah Cantrill for 100 pds 100¼ A on Wolf Island Cr, being part of 1782 grant to Charles Harris. Nov. 25, 1794. Jacob Cantrill, Isaac Cantrell.

Book E, page 303. James Galloway to Michael Rouse for 100 pds 100 A on Dan R & Adams Br adj John Miller. Dec. 16, 1798. Joshua Smith, John Minzies, Thomas Piner.

Book E, page 304. Andrew Hunter to George Russell for 1 pd 10 sh 8 A adj sd Hunter & sd Russel. Feb. 27, 1798. Peter Hunter, Wm. Motley, Richard Martin.

Book E, page 305. John Scales to Peter Scales & Daniel Scales for 25 pds 17 sh 270 A on both sides Beaver Island Cr, being part of grant to sd John Scales. Feb. 27, 1798. Robert Joyce, Joshua Smith, Robert Philips.

Book E, page 306. State of N.C. to John Smith 85 A adj John
Brown, Drury Williams, Robert Galloway Esq. Dec. 18, 1797.

Book E, page 307. Richard Sharp to Robert Burton of Granville
Co. for $500 160 A on W side Mayo R, being land devised to sd
Richard Sharp by will of John Sharp dec'd. Dec. 10, 1797. Sam
Henderson, G. Davidson.

Book E, page 308. John Matlock Esq, High Sheriff, to Samuel
Allen for 24 pds 133 A on Hogans Cr adj John Martin, Benjamin
Moore, John Wilson, being land seized & sold to highest bidder
to satisfy debt of William Bradberry to estate of John Marr dec'd.
Feb. 22, 1798. W. Bethell.

Book E, page 309. James Siers to William Jennings for 5 pds 5 A
on N side Mayo Mountain adj sd Siers & sd Jennings, Peter Hairston, Thomas Lewallin. Apr. 29, 1795. Joshua Smith, Andrew Joy,
John Smith.

Book E, page 310. James Hays to Joseph Roberts for 10 pds 50 A
on Jacobs Cr adj sd Hays, John D. Carner, Daniel Harris. Jan.
17, 1798. John Reagon, Mary Reagon.

Book E, page 311. James Galloway to Thomas Piner for 100 pds
100 A on Dan R adj Rouse, John Miller. Dec. 16, 1797. Joshua
Smith, John Menzies, Andrew Robertson.

Book E, page 312. Stephen Sanders to James Tate for 60 pds 100
A on Big Rockhouse Cr adj Abraham Philips, William P. Fowler,
Thomas Trolinger, Henry Wesbrook. Jan. 9, 1798. A. Philips,
Samuel Heath.

Book E, page 313. William Philips to Nathan Busick for 50 pds
80 A on Hogans Cr adj sd Philips, Andrew Martin. Nov. 29, 1795.
Vincent Wheeler, William Philips.

Book E, page 314. Moses Curry to Andrew Boyd for 225 pds 183 A
on Haw R adj William Jones, John Curry, Robert Curry. Nov. 17,
1797. N. Wright.

Book E, page 315. Henson Humphry to Absalom Harvey for 100 pds
140 A on Country line Cr adj Thomas Hardin, Haggard. Oct. 16,
1797. Peter Hardin, Henry Hardin.

Book E, page 316. James Higgins to Henson Humphrys for 100 pds
130 A on Haw R adj Abraham Philips, Joseph Payne, Joshuah Wright,
William Robertson, being part of 300 A grant in 1784 to sd Higgins. Oct. 14, 1793. Robert Carson, John Burk, James Taylor,
Amy Humfrey.

Book E, page 317. James Walker to Josiah Wright for 350 pds
150 A on Giles Cr adj Humphrey, being land willed to sd Wright
by his father Joshua Wright. Feb. 13, 1798. Walter Martin, J.
Charters.

Book E, page 318. State of N.C. to James Mateer 296 A on Roses
Cr adj sd Mateer, Andrew Hall, John McKibbon, Andrew Martin,
Hamilton. Dec. 11, 1797.

Book E, page 319. By order of Superior Court of Salisbury District Hubbard Peoples, Samuel Maxwell, James Coots, Watson Wharton
& John Starrol appointed Commissioners to divide & appropriate
two tracts of James Donnel late of Guilford Co. No. 1 Thomas

Donnel 240 A on North Bufflow Cr in Guilford Co. No. 2 Samuel
Donnel 482 A, part of each tract on North Buffalo and Mill Cr
crossing into Rockingham Co. adj Patrick, Parker & Cafe. Aug. 21,
1798. M. Stokes, Clerk Superior Court.

Book E, page 321. State of N.C. to Philip Gates 101 A on Jacobs
Cr adj John Chadwell. July 10, 1797.

Book E, page 322. William Nelson of Montgomery Co., Tenn. to
William Godsey for 300 pds 257 A on both sides Jacobs Cr adj
Thomas Lowe, Robert Martin, John Nelson, Moses Nelson. Dec. 3,
1798. Robert Napier, Eliza Lowe, Thomas Godsey.

Book E, page 323. Andrew Wilson & wife Margaret to Peter & John
Byzor for 300 pds 300 A on Haw R adj Cuningham, Widow Wilson.
Sept. 29, 1798. William Walker, John W. Jones, Thomas Humphreys.

Book E, page 324. James Hunter Esq, late Sheriff of Guilford Co.
to Alexander Martin Esq., Assignee for John Morton, 10 pds for
80 A, being highest bid of land of estate of Joseph Roberts dec'd
seized by Deputy John Hunter. Nov. 8, 1792. Saml. Henderson,
Hutchins Burton.

Book E, page 325. John Matlock Esq, High Sheriff, to Robert Boak
for 25 pds 260 A on Gr Rockhouse Cr & Piney Cr adj John McCarrel,
John Perkle, John King, being land seized for debt of estate of
John Marr dec'd in behalf of William Astin. Feb. 23, 1799. R.
Bethell.

Book E, page 326. John Fields & Joseph Gibson, Executors of
Joseph Gibson dec'd to Charles Norman for 101 pds 10 sh 259 A on
Buffalo Island Cr. Mar. 13, 1798. Charles Harris, Absalom Gibson.

Book E, page 326. William Hand request Sheriff John Fields to
make deed of former land of Joseph Gibson as sd Hand becomes the
purchaser from Charles Norman. Mar. 10, 1798.

Book E, page 327. Southey Griffin & wife Eley to Thomas North
for 60 pds 80 A between Lickfork and Wolf Island Cr and on Iron
Works Road. Feb. 22, 1799. William Bethell, John Smith, John
Harper.

Book E, page 328. John Joyce Sr. to Edward Eastham of Halifax
Co., Va. for 300 pds Va. money 536 A on brs of Shepherds Cr adj
James Hunter, Elijah Joyce, Thomas Cook, Benjamin Cook. Nov. 2,
1798. Nicholas Dalton, Samuel Joyce, John Dotson, Thomas Lewellen.

Book E, page 329. Isaiah Jenkins of Rowan Co. to William Walker
for 100 pds 120 A on Hogans Cr adj Baily Martin. Dec. 14, 1798.
William Martin, Bailey Martin.

Book E, page 330. John Matlock Esq, High Sherifff, to Michael
Caffey for 26 pds 100 A on Big Troublesome Cr, being land seized
to satisfy debt against estate of John Marr dec'd to William
Astin. Feb. 28, 1799.

Book E, page 331. William Farrington of Guilford to Aaron York
for 50 pds 200 A on Hogans & Jacobs Cr & both sides Johnson
Kings old road. Aug. 27, 1795. John Holladay, John Cory.

Book E, page 332. John Bellefant to Vincent Vass Jr. of Person Co. for 225 pds Va. money 310 A on Adams Br & the river adj James Ray, George Peay, Covinton, Adam Tate. Oct. 26, 1798. Geo. Peay Sr., J. Campbell, Mordicai Johnson.

Book E, page 333. Elizabeth Roberts, Exr of James Roberts dec'd to Philip Rose for 100 pds 134 A on Clouds Cr of Dan R adj sd Roberts, George Carter. Feb. 15, 1799. Sneed Strong, John Rose, Zach. Strong, Naman Roberts, Thomas Rose.

Book E, page 334. John Leak Esq to Joseph Henry Scales for $10 ½ A lot in Town of Leaksville on Henry Street, called No. 12. Feb. 25, 1799. J. Charters, Louis Winston.

Book E, page 335. John Leak Esq to John Charters for $10 136 poles on Water Street adj Town of Leaksville called lot 40. Feb. 25, 1799. Thomas Winston, J. Lenox.

Book E, page 336. John Cummings to William Simpson for 10 pds 172½ A on Jacobs Cr adj A. Martin Esq. Feb. 26, 1799. A. Philips, Sampson Lanier.

Book E, page 337. William Cayton to Dabney Carr of Henry Co., Va. for $200 ½ A lot in Town of Leaksville known as No. 5 on Henry Street. Dec. 20, 1798. James Taylor, Nathl. Scales.

Book E, page 338. Joel Foster to Henry Jackson for 50 pds 147 A on N side Waggon Road leading from Joyces Ford on Mavo R & crossing one br of Daltons Cr. Feb. 25, 1799. Joshua Smith, Thomas Smith, John Amos Jr.

Book E, page 339. State of N.C. to Abraham Glenn 200 A on Kerbys Cr adj Francis Ford, Lacy. July 16, 1795.

Book E, page 340. State of N.C. to Nathaniel Linder 100 A on Jacobs Cr adj sd Linder. July 9, 1794.

Book E, page 341. State of N.C. to Walter Martin 83 A on Bold Run Cr adj Isaac Philips, Robert Pamplin, Nathaniel Linder. July 10, 1797.

Book E, page 342. State of N.C. to Jacob Bernard, Assignee for Alexander Joyce, 19 A on Wolf Island Cr adj John Pound, Elijah Cantrill. Dec. 11, 1797.

Book E, page 343. William Paterson to John Morehead for 60 pds 100 A on Burchfields fork of Wolf Island Cr. 1798. W. Bethell.

Book E, page 344. John McKibbon Sr. to Thomas McKibbon, planter of Mecklenburg Co. for 50 pds 235 A being cheifly in Rockingham Co. on Roases and Giles Crs adj John Cunningham, Nicholas Smith. Feb. 29, 1799. Thomas Webb, John McKibbon.

Book E, page 345. George Peay Sr. to Dr. John C. Cox for $20 ½ A lot in Town of Leaksville on Henry Street known as lot No. 2. Feb. 6, 1799.

Book E, page 346. John London Esq of Georgia to Joseph New comb for 50 pds part of a tract of land adj sd London, Collo. Wilson, on a County Road from A. Yarbrough to Rockingham Courthouse along road to Sorrow Town Road. Dec. 16, 1790. James Akin, John Odineal.

Book E, page 347. James Watt to Thomas Key for 100 pds 246 A on Hogans Cr where sd Key now lives adj Bean, Nat Williams. Sept. 3, 1798. Thomas Certain, Saml. Watt.

Book E, page 348. John May, former Sheriff to George Washington Lent Marr, John Marr Jr., William Miller Marr, Constant Hardin Marr and Peter Nicholas Marr, being lawful heirs of John Marr dec'd of Henry Co., Va. 260 A on SE side Dan R adj Daniel Dotson, being land on which John Hunter dec'd lived, being seized and sold in 1788 by direction of his will to executors to pay off debt to Sarah Scott, with John Marr, now dec'd being the highest bidder of 200 pds. (Last part of deed missing.)

102

Brewer cont.
John 37
Sarah 6
Bridge, Thomas 94
Briggs, Elisha 22,40,47
Margaret 40
Brim, John 89,95
Joseph 17
Rice 17,54
Brison, John 18
James 51
Brochus, John 42
Brock, Brooks, George 39,
43
George 39,43
Humphy 59,89,90
Sharod 1,5,7,8
Thomas 38
Umphry 46,59
Brown, Alexander 2,21,41,
57,59,66,71,72,74,81
David 60
Elijah 47,48,53
George 41,68,81,87
Hugh 57,61
James 21,38,41,60,61,71,
77,78,82,86,95
James Sr. 36,77
John 36,61,63,65,86,94,
98
Joshua 10
Margaret 61
Robert 13,40,57,61,76
Robert A. 65
Samuel 24,30,57,61,77,
90
Stephen 13
Thomas 42
William 10,60,77,86
Browder, ... 42,52,78
Augustine 88
Isham 22,23,28,29,76
Jesse 3
John 52,70,76
Letitha 48
Talith 58,70
Widdow 29,42,43
Bruce, Charles 4,22,42,46,
52,56,64,68,73,85,93,
94
Elizabeth 89
George 41
James 31
Thomas 31,41
Brunt, Thomas 67
Bryant, Ashon 20
Zachariah 17,24,30,56
Buchanon, John 17
Widow 88
William 21,29,45,51,79,
82,87,90
Burch, Borch, Henry 18,52,
54
Pemberton 10
Robert 12
Susanna 54
Burford, Dan 44
Bull, Severangan 17
Burk, Bourk, John 55,65,
98
William 44,48
Burn, Burns, John 3
James 91
Burnett, George 58
Burton, ... 9,32
David 10,28
Edmund 36,44
Hutchins 99
John 8
Joseph 2,6,13,21,24
Robert 1,9,98
Richard 32
William 24

Busick, Nathan 98
Butt, Severingan 84
Swerangon 50
Byrd, Bird, ... 69
Elizabeth 1
William 1
Bysor, John 99
Peter 99

Caffey, Coffey, Coffee
John 32,35,75,76,78
Joshua 76,77
Michael 15,21,22,32,35,
49,61,70,88,99
Thomas 32
Calbreath, Alexander 34
Caldwell, Colwell, David
21,39
William 6,88
Calhoun, Samuel 81
Callahan, Calahan, Calaham
Darby 10,14,37,94
Edward 69
Ezekiel 8,35,41,69
James 69
Jane 69
Nathaniel 69
Unity 69
Calland, Samuel 63
Callaway, Doshea 51
Caller, Frederich 28
Campbell, ... 35,75
J. 100
James 2,12,13,66,68,83,
94
John 23
Moses 29,46,59,68
Patrick 57
Cannon, Lettice
Minos 28,29,41
William 79
Cantrell, Cantrill,
Aaron 4,5,58,70
Charles 14,15,16,97
Elijah 70,77,89,94,97,
100
Elisha 93
Isaac 3,15,21,40,42,43,
47,49,60,75,93,97
Jacob 16,41,47,49,58,65,
70,78,89,97
James 17,60,70
John 23,29,43,49,52,58
Robert 14,16
Sampson 52
Thomas 45
Cardwell, Daniel 91
Nathan 77,91
Richard 8,45,74
William 73
Carman, John 16
Carner, John D. 41,71,98
John Daniel 68
Carr, Dabney 100
Elizabeth 52
John Fendel 52,54,80
Thomas 92
Carrico, Abel 94
William 92
Carson, Robert 98
Carter, George 10,14,19,
100
Giles 90
Maria 76
Presley 14
Thomas 34,59
Cartwright, William 75,81,
90
Caruthers, James 7,77
Martha 4,7
Case, William 52,60,68,80,
91
Cash, Howard 72

Cavender, Ezekiel 13
Cayton, Caton, Jacob 11,20
William 84,85,92,100
Certain, Sertain, Thomas
37,88,101
Chadwell, John 7,49,67,79,
96,99
Challes, Henry 94
Hugh 1,22,59
John 24,25,65,67,83,89,
90
Chamber, Chambers, Fanne
10
Phebe 39
Thomas 10,11,14,18,19,
38,39,58
William 10,11,14,18,19,
20
Chambless, Chambles, ...46
Henry 16
Chanie, Chane, ... 14
Fanne 14
Rebeckah 10
Chapman, Joseph 9
Thomas 33
William Sr. 33
William Jr. 33
Charters, J. 65,98,100
John 100
Chinault, Shenault, Abner
1,64
Childres, Stephen 5
Churton, William 69
Clark, ... 42
David 13
Isaac 23,24,31,35,48,50,
63,76,89,96
Joseph 15,23,29,31,32,
43,48,50,69,76,77,80,
96
Margaret 96
Nancy 69,77
Thomas 32
William 10,32,41,50,51,
52,67,96
William Sr. 35
William Jr. 23,24,61
Claybrook, James 56,66
Clegg, Sarah 62,63
Clemens, James 44
Clendenin, Joseph 6
Clifton, John 56
Cloud, Benjamin 7
Joseph 1,7,15,30
William 7
Cobler, Kobler, Christop-
her 12,42,43
Frederich 12,27
Cochran, Benjamin 43
Reuben 26,76
William 76
Cockrill, Cockrell,
Francis 83
Jacob 11
Lewis 39,57,83
William 8,11,26,30,39,
56,83
Cole, Robert 30
Coleman, ... 69,73
James 14
Robert 16,31,85
William 16
Colley, James 36
Maynard 35,41
Collings, Chas. 27
Collins, William 21,30,37
Coleson, Coulson, Colson
..... 14
George 6,9,81
Henry 49,97
Thomas 82
Colton, James 4,13
Colquitt, James 17

Harbour, John 59
Harden, Hardin, Harding
• Henry 5,7,28,31,37,51,
    53,64,67,93,98
  Jeremiah 67
  John 17
  M. 2,59
  M. Jr. 25,27,39
  Mark 7,51
  Mark Sr. 11,20
  Peter 93,98
  Thomas 23,28,31,53,72,
    93,98
  William 78
Hardister, Benjamin 83
Harkins, Hugh 2,3,5,11,19,
    20,24,27,35,50,60,62,
    64
  James 70
  Sarah 27
Harmon, John 78
  Sarah 78
Harper, John 43,44,54,57,
    75,83,86,87,99
  Margaret 83
Harris, Hairis, ... 3,
    20,44,48,82
  Charles 2,6,13,14,28,
    29,43,97,99
  Daniel 98
  Hanah 33,64,78
  Jesse 1,5,8,27,41,69
  John 13,20,29,41,58,69,
    70,71,78,87,89,95
  Leaven 69,71,95
  Lucey 31
  Nathaniel 1,8,12,41,43,
    58
  Robert 28,31,43,58
  Simpson 28,66
  Thomas 1,31,34,58,86
  Tyre 20,28
  William 68,71,92
Harrison, ... 28
  Charles 96
  Elijah 27,36
  James 4,90
  Jesse 33
  John 89
  Nathaniel 13,35
  Richard 11
  William 31,34,41,47,62,
    65
Harvey, Absalom 93,98
Hatfield, Thomas 48,62
Hatrick, Robert 62,65,74
Hawkins, Samuel Bower 65,
    66
Hayes, Hays, Hay, ...56,
    87
  Henry 8,11,13,14,24
  Js. 3
  James 3,5,12,13,36,37,
    38,39,55,61,70,91,93,
    96,98
  James Sr. 64,77
  James Jr. 46,71,77,79
  John 14,40,93
  Margaret 14
  Nancy 8,24
  Patrick 3,22
  Thomas 48
  William 35,93
Haley, Hayley, James 93,
    97
Heath, John 90,93
  Samuel 98
Heather, Adam 3
Henderson, ... 13,73,91
  Fanny 51
  James 45
  Michael 8
  Pleasant 1,71,73,91

Henderson cont.
  Richard 20,23,30,36,45,
    50,60,61
  Samuel 5,34,43,51,56,72,
    73,76,91,98,99
  Susan 1
  Thomas 2,6,8,9,13,15,16,
    18,20,23,26,27,30,37,
    39,54,62,64,66,67,69,
    72,76,78,79,82,84,85,
    95,96
Hendrick, Hendricks, Abra-
    ham 57
  Henry 38,39,49,56
  John 58
  Walter 83
  William 58
Hendrickson, ... 16
  Abraham 25,29,54
  Henry 65
  John 21
Henry, Rebecca 64
Herbin, Harbin, George 89
  John 21,62,65,84,89
  John Jr. 56
  William 61,62,65,84,89
Herrin, Herron, Herring
  John 14,17,38,41,44,47,
    67
  Samuel 38,59,70,75,83
Hewlett, Patsey 97
Hickman, ... 31,78
  John 32
  William 9,11,14,32,73
Higgins, James 7,35,44,48,
    98
Highland, Dominick 16,30,
    32,55
Hill, Cager 40
  Gustavis 96
  Isaac 90
  James 9
  John 8,9,25,54,59,78
  Moses 96
  Samuel 40
  Thomas S. 5
  Walter 35,42,59,61,75
  William 5,9,88,96
  Rev. William 59
Hingson, Kingson
  Richard 50,55,70,77,79
Hinton, Jesse 36,42,43,57,
    77
Hitchcock, William 34
Hodge, ... 65,67,68,92
  Francis 40,45,60
  James 47,60,71,77
  John 3,8,14,19,53,68,94
  John Charles 60,94,95
  William 60,79,94
Haggard, Hoggard, ... 28,
    98
  Benjamin 39,59,71
  Edmund 26,27,85
  William 74
Hoggates, Nathaniel 29
Hogge, John 22
Holderness, Frances 25
  James 6,13,16,25,27
  J. 4,13
Holgan, Holgin, Thomas 6,
    8,11,12,16,21,24,30,
    32,39,50
Holker, Adam 2,5,19
Hollowday, John 49
Hollock, John 15,16,29
Holloway, John 92
Hollowell, Asa 88,94
Holmes, John 53,83,88
Holt, Bud 85
  Mary 90
  William 85
Hooper, Enos 4

Hopkins, Richard 47
  Solomon 79
Hopper, Darby 69
  Jenna 53
  John 69
  Joseph 27,29,42,43,53,
    57,77,85
  Joshua 11,37,59,94
  Lewis 57
  Thomas 11
  William 27,29
Hopwood, James 71
Hornbuckle, George 27,67,
    •72,93
  Jane 68,72
  Thomas 53
  William 27,28,53,61,68,
    72
Horsford, Elizabeth 64,70,
    87
  James 11,12,25,58
  John 11,33,38,58,63,64,
    70,87,97
Howard, William 63
Howell, Betsy 55
  John 29,55,66
  John Sr. 68
  Thomas 84
Howerton, Fanney 24
  Obadiah 70
Howlet, William 14
Hubbard, Hubbart, Hurrert
    56
  Easter 42
  Esther 57
  Widow 55
  William 9,16,26,36,37,
    42,46,48,50,57,68,76
Hudson, Robert 81
Hughes, Hughs, ... 19
  Archelaus 3
  Archibald 69
  Terry 92
Humphreys, Humphrey, Hum-
    frey
  Amy 98
  Elizabeth 48
  John 33,48
  Hinson 67
  Hans. 85,89
  Henson 98
  Thomas 99
Hunt, William 21,45,67,81
Hunter, ... 26,34,35
  Alexander 95
  Andrew 51,97
  Edward 2
  George 39,46,51,59,90
  James 9,19,25,27,34,36,
    45,49,53,69,97,99
  John 6,8,15,37,39,46,51,
    66,67,70,74,76,82,90,
    95,99,101
  John Jr. 10,16,19,31
  Peter 39,46,90,91
  Samuel 32,97
Hussey, John 6
Hutchings, Drewry 17
Hutson, Robert 45,62
Hyler, David 82,89

Irion, Charlotte 25
  Frederich 80
  Lewis 25
  Phil. 45
  Philip Jacob 18
Irvin, Ervin, James 97
  Jean 72
  Joseph 57

Jackson, Henry 100
  James 16,49,52,55,88,91

Jackson cont.
  Reuben 18,52,54
  Thomas 52,55
James, Abraham 1,5,7,8,41
  Elizabeth 38
  Emanuel 70,88
  Isaac 5,8,41
  Jacob 1,5,7,8
  Susanna 5
  Thomas 15,38,53
  William 1,5,8,41,43
Jamison, Thomas 3,39,81,
    83
Jenkins, Isaiah 99
  James 61
  Joseph 51
  Philip 15
Jennings, William 63,85,
    92,94,98
  William Crunk 51
Johnson, Johnston - (No
  way to separate these two
  families for indexing with-
  out genealogical study)
  Abner 5,16
  Alexander 94
  Gabriel 1
  Gideon 3,5,10,16,29,38,
    46,63
  Gideon Sr. 11,20,97
  James 15,21,50
  Joel 48,53,60
  John 31,51,53,60
  Joseph Pain 9,29
  Lancelott 65
  Lewis Hobby 26
  Mordicai 100
  Peter 10,16
  Sarah 38
  Thomas 65
  William 5,10,16,17,34,
    38,39,46,59,63,78
Joyce, Joice
  Alexander 48,50,52,53,
    54,55,58,60,61,63,66,
    74,76,80,84,93,94,100
  Andrew 4,8,37,40,62,85,
    98
  Black Smith John 8
  Delilah 18
  Elijah 4,5,37,51,71,85,
    92,99
  Elisha 5,7,50,84
  George 18,73
  James 18,61
  Joe T. 54
  John 4,8,9,12,18,33,40,
    49,51,71,74,92,94,97
  John Sr. 94
  Joseph T. 64,68,91
  Martha 91
  Nancy 92
  Robert 50,64,71,73,74,
    85,86,92,94,97
  Samuel 99
  Thomas 6,40,64,71,72,
    82,91
  William 74
Jones, Dudley 86
  Edmund 38
  Ezekiel 40,57,64,78,80
  George 81
  James 5,19
  John 7,8,17,24,26,44,
    45,46,61,62,63,67,87,
    90
  John Wheeler 85,86
  John W. 55,82,99
  Mary 16
  Robert 27
  Robert Jr. 1,2,40
  Thomas 87

Jones cont.
  William 3,13,15,16,17,
    24,29,30,32,39,40,41,
    42,47,54,55,56,61,62,
    66,67,68,71,72,73,74,
    78,81,82,85,88,98
  William Jr. 39,75
  William Sr. 71,87
Jordan, Jordon, James 11
  Notley 1,34,39
  Polley 39
Judge, George 54,76,91

Kallam, Kellum, Callom
  Spencer 46,81,90
  William 9,24,33,35,46,
    59,75,81,88,91,93
  William Sr. 26
Kello, Isaac 4,9,68
Kelley, Dennis 24,38
  James 35,36,46,59
  William 45
Kerr, Jesse 80,89
Kewes, William 9
Key, Mary 61
  Thomas 28,37,38,43,61,88
Kilman, Kilmon, Henry 70,
    78,82,94
Kimble, Kimbol, George 21,
    31,42,74
Kimbrell, ... 21
Kimbrough, Robert 55,66,86
King, Henry 25,62,64,79
  John 71,97,99
  Johnson 77,99
  Lemire 77
  Levy 21,59,69,75
  Peter 20,24
  Thomas 2,7,23,25,28,29,
    36,46,72,77,88
  Thomas Sr. 35,41,71
  Thomas Jr. 38,79,95
  William 55
  Zachariah 52,55,82
Kingson see Hingson
Kilpatrick, Hugh 5,32,37
  Sarah 5,93,95
Knight, Sampson 3
  Thomas 50,80
Kobler see Cobler

Lacy, ... 54,100
  B.C. 18,70
  Batte C. 45,63,91
  Batte Cocke 23,43
  Elizabeth 91
  Hopkins 23,39,45
  John 23,45,89
  M. 97
  Theophelus 23,43,45,91,
    97
  William 23,45,76,89
Ladd, Constantine 49
  Joseph 2,66,77
  Mary 49
Land, Moses 35
Lane, Lain, ... 20,22,
    31,38,60
  Rachel 60
  Samuel 16
Langford, William 3,6
Lanier, Caterine 36
  Elizabeth 40
  Henry 30,37,40,54
  Isham 13,36,39
  James 23,37,39,40
  Mary 40
  Nathaniel 8,20,36,42
  Sampson 31,40,66,81,83,
    84,100
  Samuel 34
  Thompson 36,68

Larimore, Larrimore, ...
    83
  Elizabeth 59
  H. 62
  Hance 49,54
  Nicholas 23,45,49,76
  Philamon 30
  Philip 24
  Richard 30
  Robert 58,62
  Samuel 49
Larkin, Lerkin, Thomas 23,
    25,29,31,35,77,88
Lawson, Nath. 11
  William 1
Leak, James 9
  John 2,4,5,7,26,43,51,
    62,74,80,84,90,92,93,
    100
Leathers, Michael 23,32,
    80
Leekey, William 50
Leigh, Richard 7,9
Lemons, Lemon, Lemonds,
    Leoman
  Elizabeth 35
  George 3,9,40,57,60,92
  John 20,35,40,41,57,85,
    88
  John Sr. 74,82
  John Jr. 74,82
  Joseph 41,57
  William 3,35,47,64
Lewis, Andrew 81
  John 9,14,28,40,60,66,
    71
  Morris 92
  Peter 34,53
  Sarah 26,63,73
  Shadrack 33
  Thomas 81
  William 6,47
  Wm. L. 13
  William Lankston 8,25,
    26,54
Lephew, Sephew, Stephen
    12,17,24,46,82,89
Lenox, J. 100
  John 54,65,66
Lewellen, Lewellin, Thomas
    63,98,99
  Thomas Sr. 94
  Thomas Jr. 94
Lilley, Robert 42,69,85,
    88
Linder, John 15,21,22,29,
    42,43,44,48,52,62,66,
    84,95
  Joseph 36
  Mary 15,25,28,29,57,77,
    92
  Nathaniel 2,7,24,25,26,
    28,29,31,38,40,41,42,
    43,46,47,50,52,54,55,
    57,59,60,62,63,64,66,
    70,74,77,81,87,92,100
Loftis, Job 9,10,11,14,32,
    34,59
  Solomon 26,76
  William 13,16
Loman, Loaman, George 95
  John 46
Lomax, Elizabeth 49
  James 37,77
  Marget 92
  Moses 49,68,84,87,92
  Robert 92
  Thomas 21,22,39,43,49,
    55,57,60,68,77,84,87,
    92
  Thomas Jr. 68
  William 87

Robson, Thomas 8
Rogers, James 15
  Thomas 57,79
Rolston, Rollstone, Isaac
  22,37,93
  Robert 37,93
Rouse, ... 98
  Michael 97
Rose, ... 14
  James 63
  John 100
  Philip 10,19,26,30,46,
    69,100
  Samuel 27
  Thomas 26,30,100
Ross, Philip 7,90
  Reubin 90
  Robertson 90
  Robinson 68
Rossell, Rossel, Rosell
  Richard 68,79,82,91
Rowland, Roland, ... 49
  Benjamin 61
  David 55,61,73
  George 12,19,24,35,39,
    42,55,61,62,70,73,78
  James 61
  John 41,55,61,73
Ruson, John 16,55,56
Russell, Russel
  Alexander 64
  George 97
  Rachel 89
  Robert 52
  Samuel 68
  William 1,5,39,44,59,62,
    71,94
Russey, James 81
  Sarah 81

Sallerabet, James 9
Samuel, Augustin 92,93
Saunders, Sanders,
  Elizabeth 59
  Henry 60,87,89
  James 5,15,17,24,30,49,
    56,57,59,74,80
  James Jr. 74
  John 78
  Robert 26,30
  Stephen 56,98
  William 89
Savage, Elizabeth 15,31
  John 27
  Thomas 31
  Widdow 30,42
  William 21,27,28,31,34
  Zebidee 58
  Zebulin 28,30,31
Scales, Daniel 97
  David 25,82
  Henry 3,4,12,13,17,25,
    26,28,35,59,78,88,94
  James 5,6,23,73,81,82,
    91
  J. H. 97
  John 18,32,97
  Joseph 6,18,63,83
  Joseph Henry 100
  Nathaniel 10,12,20,90,
    97,100
  Peter 18,85,97
Scarbrough, James 95
Scogin, Scroggin, John 6,
  13,14,16,17
Scott, ... 35
  Andrew 20,21,24,27,60
  David 20,24
  Edward 4,16,48
  Joe 88
  John 97
  Joseph 80,97
  Sarah 48,101

Scott cont.
  Thomas 42,49,55,74,81
  William 55
Scurry, Widow 84
Searcy, T. 26,29,67,73
  Thomas 8,17,62,95
Self, William 37
Senior, Seancr, Bryant 42,
  80
Serin, Thomas 38
Sertain see Certain
Settle, ... 12
  Benjamin 4,65,66,72,79
  David 26,27,36,37,38,39,
    45,48,60,63,65,66,67,
    68,72,78,79,95
  Edward 72
  Jemima 66
  John 54
  Josiah 64,65,66,70,72,
    76,79
  Mary 72
  Thomas 60
Shackleford, Elizabeth 29,
  89
  Isham 1,73,82
  James 82
  John 98
  Rachel 89
  Richard 1,6,19,29,40,49,
    73,98
  Salley 89
  Samuel 74
  William 92
Shaw, Ralph 14,44
Shelton, Elijah 44
  John 44,68
  Joseph 76
  Samuel 76,82
Shenault see Chinault
Shepherd, John 23,28,67,79
Shickle, Charles 60,83
Shippen, Elizabeth Carter
  75,76
  Thomas Lee 75
  W. Jr. 76
Short, Aron 48
  Moses 41,68,71
  Moses Sr. 68
  Samuel 22,42,68,72,79,
    85,94
  Widow 39
  William 62
  William Oldham 39,41,45,
    49,67
Shropshire, Winkfield 32
Siers, Alse 7
  Enuch 7
  James 63,94,98
  Jesse 7,24
Sillevan, Sillavant,
  Daniel 14,28
  William 68,81
Silman, Benjamin 4,12,17
  John 22,54
  William 35
Simmons, Simons, Simon
  Elisha 69,97
  Elizabeth 42
  George 45
  Isham 24,42,69,85
  John 11,16,17,19,27,30,
    31,41,42,56,62,69,81,
    85,86
  John Jr. 27,31,46
  Salley 27
Simpson, David 93
  Peter 87
  R. 28
  Richard 65,93
  Richard Jr. 42
  Thomas 42,85
  William 100

Sims, Simms, James 5
  John 15,74,84
  Mary 26
  Mathew 8,9,25,26
  Thomas 91
Sithes, Josiah 10
Skinner, Charles 83
  Joshua 92
  Sarah 56
  Thomas 45,56
Slydeln, Samuel 17
Small, Elizabeth 38
  Robert 3,6,25,29,37,38,
    43,54,56,59,61,71,79,
    95,97
Smith, Ben 94
  Ben Dawson 80
  Benjamin 33,54,73,81,82,
    84
  Charles 35
  Drury 4,33,35,48,65,66,
    73,80,93
  Elizabeth 35
  Gordon 4,57
  James 30,31,49,86,87
  John 1,4,5,12,22,30,33,
    49,59,60,62,66,67,69,
    71,74,76,80,89,94,98,
    99
  Joshua 5,6,7,8,9,12,13,
    18,24,25,27,28,33,35,
    40,43,45,46,50,51,53,
    54,56,62,64,66,73,74,
    76,78,82,84,85,88,90,
    94,97,98,100
  Lemuel 3,6
  Lurania 84
  Martha 42
Smith, Mathew 89
  Samuel 16,42,62
  Sarah 28
  Sarah Sr. 26
  Sarah Jr. 26
  Thomas 93,100
  William 7,66
  Zachariah 4
Sneed, Alexander 54,71,78,
  85
  Zach 59
Somerhays, Robert W. 33
Southern, Reuben 26
Sparks, Elizabeth 96
  Jeremiah 18,25
  Mary 25
  Milley 25
  Thomas 7,15,25,33,67,
    87,89,96
  Thomas Jr. 82
Spears, Spiers, Spirse
  William 16,19,23,28,34,
    35,44,78,86
Spencer, Abraham 36,86
  Benjamin 27,30,33,50,55,
    62,65,84
  John 50,84,87,97
  Thomas 49,84
Spragins, Milchejah 23
Sprout, ... 12
  James 39,42,74
  John 42,61,73
Spurrier, John 65
  Theophilus 65
Stacy, Stephen 81,88
Standard, William 56,93
Stanford, Elizabeth 64
  John 15,21,29,35,42,45,
    61,62,64,86,87,88
  Nancy 64
Stanley, Standley,
  Zachariah 5,10,16,19
Stapleton, William 43,80
Starrat, Starrot, Starrol
  John 82,83,98

Stephens, John 2
  Peter 48
  Sarah 29
  Widow 95
  William 17,70
Stepts, William 8
Stewart, Steward, James
    75
  John 3,27,49
  Richard 80
  William 6
Still, Elizabeth 84
  Joseph 84,87
Stockard, Stockird, ...
    53
  John 41,45,50,52,55,68,
    87
Stokes, Joel 54
Stone, Benjamin 4,29
  Burger 66,89
  John 97
Strange, Fanny 77
  James 77
  John 79
Stratton, Mary 30,56
  William 42,74,67,80,91
Street, Joseph 62,66
Strong, Elizabeth 16,26,
    80
  James 8,40,94
  John 16,17,40,63,66,80,
    82,88,95
  Sneed 10,19,37,46,63,85,
    100
  Thomas 96
  Zach 84,100
Stubblefield, ... 30
  Edward 22
  Fanny 58
  Richard 1,25,31,32,56,
    58
  Theodrick 31,58
  William 2,15,43
  Wyatt 1,10,22,25,30,38,
    48
Summers, Somers, James 25,
    72
  George 72
Sumner, Holland 76
Suter, Sutor, Sewter
  John 67
  William Elliott 67
Sutherland, Southerland
  John 17,40
  William 1,40,56,63,74,
    82
Swail, Simon 76
Swift, Flower 18,25,34
  Priscilla 34
  Vinea 34

Tackett, John 4
Tankersley, George 5
Tate, Adam 9,22,38,39,48,
    55,100
  Ann 56
  James 98
  Joseph 9,40,45
  Woody 56
Tatum, Absolum 31
  Elizabeth 59
  Nathaniel 14,43,54
Taylor, Edward 15,20,41,
    58
  Horford 80,87
  James 2,48,61,74,75,80,
    87,89,90,98,100
  John 20,21,23,26,27
  John Horford 41,43,49,
    75,89
  John Louis 2
  William 16,42,80
Teary, Peter 2

Terrill, Jo. 31
Thacker, ... 42
  Charles 78
  Jeremiah 10,11,20,78,87
  Mary Ann 87
  Nathan 30,33,63,64
  Susanah 33
  Usler 78
  Zackariah 33,58
Thadesis, John 87
Thomas, ... 62
  Bryant 72
  George 13,67
  James 67
  Jesse 6,23
  Joel 23
  John 21,65,67,88,96
  Lewis 72,73,95
  Luci 29,67
  Michael 17,23,46
  Richard 70
  Senia 13
  Walker 85
  William 9,23,73,74,95
Thompson, Thomson, Thomason
  Allis 45
  Daniel 35
  Edward 52,56,78
  Epraim 89
  Gentry 39,42,43,80
  James 34,45
  John 19,30,42,62,80
  Lemuel 35
  Robert 55
  Samuel 55
  Thomas 55,57,64,68,71,88
  Wm. Ferguson 28
  William Ferr 19
Thrasher, ... 15,25,33
  Cloud 66,70
  Isaac 15,58
  Jas. C. 15
  John 52,53,56,58,86
  John Sr. 15
  John Jr. 15
  John C. 17
  Joseph C. 1
  Joseph Cloud 56,70
  Margaret 70
  Richard 32
Thornburn, James 84
Thorp, Thorpe, Joseph 81
  William 29,54,66,89
Thweatt, James 95
Tickle, Tickel, William 37,
    43
Todd, Samuel 45
Tomlinson, James 9,32,60
  John 9,31,32,60
Toney, Charles 2,18,24
  Sherwood 6,58,86,89
Torrant, Manlove 11,19,76
Tourant, Henry 58
Toteson, Lidda 53
Tramill, William 6,12,15,
    47
Tranum, Trannum, Traynem
  William 31,41,43,49,56,
    58,86,89
Trent, Alexander 81,82,84
  Field 82
Triplet, John 28
Trolinger, Adam 52,87
  Michael 2,75
  Samuel 70,77,84,87
  Thomas 98
Tronett, William 6
Trotter, Philip 1
Turner, George Sears 90
  Hester 90
  Martha 90
  Mary 90
  Tho. Geo. Richard 90

Turner cont.
  Widow 21
Twomey, Patrick 70,83
Tyler, Reubin 10

Underwood, Howell 80

Vandergriff, Vandergraph
    27
  Christopher 9,55,61,73,
    82
Vanlandingham, George 5
  Richard 74
Vass, Vincent Jr. 100
Vaughn, Vaughan, Vaun
  David 12,13,26,43,60,
    76,96
  Gideon 43
  John 19
  Sarah 13,67
Vawter, Vaughters, John
    36,46,73,91
Vermilion, Rachel 47
  Guy 13,47,65,90
Vernon, ... 8,54
  Elinor 12,13
  Elizabeth 18
  Isaac 4,18,64,80
  James 7,12,13,40
  Jane Coldwell 90
  Joanna 28
  John 18,64,74,90
  Jonathon 90
  Joseph 18
  Mary 73
  Nancy 18
  Nehemiah 4,6,18,40,62,
    64,73,74,77,81,90,92,
    93
  Nelley 7
  Obadiah 74
  Richard 6,12,18,23,47,
    72,73,74,80,90,92,94
  Robert 7
  Sarah Sims 73,90
  Thomas 18
Vincent, Moses 25

Wade, Elisha 84,85
Wafford, Waford, Waughford
  J. 52
  John 21,27,36,49,53,62,
    67,70,71,75,81,82,97
Walker, ... 20,26,80
  A. 88
  A. B. 89
  Abner 90
  Adam 3
  Alexander 13,35,47,61,
    67,79
  Allen 11,20,38,63
  David 16,35,65,73
  Elmore 2,33,84,85
  James 5,7,13,29,32,33,
    34,45,47,54,67,82,83,
    84,98
  Joab 5
  Joel 38,53,54
  John 20,24,34,74,94
  Mary 6,51
  Robert 22,23,40,42,65,
    66,78
  Warren 83
  William 17,19,23,29,31,
    33,35,38,44,52,67,76,
    82,86,99
  William Sr. 6
Wall, ... 4,22
  Claiborn 81
  Henry 52,56
  John 16,66
  Peter 66
  Robert 89,90

115

9780893083519